DOING

the

RIGHT
THING

Also by Scott B. Rae

Moral Choices: An Introduction to Ethics

Beyond Integrity: A Judeo-Christian Approach to Business Ethics (with Kenman L. Wong)

DOING

the

RIGHT
THING

MAKING MORAL CHOICES
IN A WORLD FULL OF OPTIONS

SCOTT B. RAE

ZONDERVAN®   the Colson Center™
Christian Worldview Series

ZONDERVAN

Doing the Right Thing
Copyright © 2013 by Chuck Colson Center for Christian Worldview

This title is also available as a Zondervan ebook.
Visit www.zondervan.com/ebooks.

This title is also available in a Zondervan audio edition.
Visit www.zondervan.fm.

Requests for information should be addressed to:

Zondervan, *Grand Rapids, Michigan* 49530

Library of Congress Cataloging-in-Publication Data

Rae, Scott B.
    Doing the right thing / Scott B. Rae.
    pages cm.
    ISBN 978-0-310-51399-5 (softcover)
    1. Christian ethics. 2. Christian life. I. Title.
  BJ1251.R235 2013
  241—dc23   2013013068

Cover design: *Michelle Lenger*
Interior design: *David Conn*

Printed in the United States of America

HB 01.06.2023

The book
is dedicated
to the memory
of Chuck Colson
and done in his honor

Contents

Foreword

ROBERT P. GEORGE AND MELISSA MOSCHELLA

"Be ready always with an answer to everyone who asks a reason for the hope that is in you" (1 Peter 3:15). The apostle Peter addressed these words of exhortation to the Christian communities of Asia Minor living in the midst of a hostile pagan culture. Their salience for Christians in America today could not be greater. We too live in a culture starkly at odds with Christian values, and ever more aggressively so. We too are called to give witness to our faith not only with words but also with upright moral conduct — even when that conduct clashes with the relativism and hedonism that surround us, and even at the risk of persecution. And we too are called to play our part in transforming our culture, bringing our laws and customs into line with the deep truth that each and every human being has inherent and equal dignity — a truth revealed by God but also accessible to human reason.

To be able to live as coherent Christians in today's world, we need the intellectual tools that will enable us to determine what the right thing to do is in complex situations. Moreover, to be able to explain and defend moral truths — in conversations with relatives, friends, neighbors and colleagues, and also in discussions and debates in the public square — we need to speak a language that everyone, including nonbelievers, can understand. For both of these tasks, *reason* is indispensable. That is why this book, and the DVD series that it accompanies, are so valuable. They approach morality primarily from the perspective of natural law — that is, from the perspective of what reason can tell us about which choices, actions, attitudes, and habits respect and promote human dignity and genuine human flourishing , and which do not.

Natural law is, in its most basic outlines, written by God on the human heart — that's why at some level, everyone understands that things like murder, rape, and slavery are wrong. Yet not all of the requirements of natural law are so obvious. The natural law's prohibition on killing innocent human beings is evident to all but the psychopath, but the application of that prohibition to the unborn, to human embryos, and to the severely debilitated is not. Careful study and reasoning are necessary to understand and explain why abortion, embryo-destructive research, and physician-assisted suicide are wrong, reasoning of the sort found in chapter 4 of this book. Most people who accept these forms of killing as legitimate — who have bought in to what John Paul II called the "culture of death" — have simply never heard or given serious consideration to the opposing arguments. Informing ourselves and then speaking out — respectfully but boldly — can have a powerful effect.

Doing so, of course, requires not only knowledge, but also courage, along with a host of other virtues. Morality is not only about "rules" or norms — although norms of upright conduct are among the most important moral truths — but also involves the cultivation of a virtuous character, the formation of good habits that train our will and emotions, enabling us to know and do the good — and live by valid norms that specify what it means to respect the integral human good — in a constant and reliable way. It is within the family that this training in virtue primarily takes place. As Aristotle says in the *Nicomachean Ethics*, "It makes no small difference whether we form habits of one kind or another from early youth." If we are concerned about moral decline within our cultural and its devastating effects — economic collapse, political corruption, juvenile crime, out-of-wedlock pregnancy, etc. — then we need to be concerned first and foremost with strengthening the institution of marriage as the foundation of healthy family life.

And here too is another area in which it is crucial that Christians be capable of giving reason-based arguments to defend this vital yet beleaguered institution.

In a 1953 letter, C. S. Lewis proposes the following line of attack for the moral and religious decay he perceived in the culture of his time: "For my part I believe we ought to work not only at spreading the Gospel (that certainly) but also at a certain preparation for the Gospel. It is necessary to recall many to the law of nature *before* we talk about God. For Christ promises forgiveness of sins: but what is that to those who, since they do not know the law of nature, do not know that they have sinned? Who will take medicine unless he knows he is in the grip of disease? Moral relativity is the enemy we have to overcome before we tackle Atheism." If these words were true in the 1950s, how much more so in our own day! Christians must fight doggedly against the moral relativism that saps the vital energy of our culture. This book and accompanying DVD series are powerful arms for the battle.

Introduction

*D*oing the Right Thing is a companion book to the film series by the same name produced by Chuck Colson. This film series was the last great project to which Chuck devoted himself. He wanted very much to make a difference in ethics in the culture, for he believed that a society that honors religious freedom is dependent on virtue being deeply rooted in that culture. He was alarmed at the breakdown in moral standards in our country and the rise of relativism — the way in which people either ignore morality or make up their own moral rules — all without giving thought to the incoherence of such a way of life.

Chuck's heart for ethics came in large part from his long-time study of the life of William Wilberforce, the eloquent, late-eighteenth through early-nineteenth-century British member of Parliament who gave his life to two primary goals — the abolition of slavery in the British Empire and what he called "the reformation of manners."[1] By manners, he meant a reformation of ethics and morality in British culture. Life for most people in the teeming cities of the newly industrialized England in Wilberforce's day was crude, as chronicled by Charles Dickens in his novels. Chuck likewise saw the decline in moral standards in the United States and produced the film series in an attempt to make a difference in the ethical landscape in our culture.

But Chuck's heart for ethics did not come just from his study of the great heroes of the Christian faith like Wilberforce. It also came from his thirty-five years of work in our nation's prison system. Prison Fellowship, the ministry to inmates that he founded shortly after he was released from prison for his role in the Watergate scandal, provided him with the life experience that drove his interest in ethics. After interviewing countless inmates and spending years studying the various factors that contributed to a person's incarceration, Chuck concluded that the one thing nearly all inmates had in common was not their backgrounds, family dysfunction, or poverty; it was rather that they had all made poor moral choices that ultimately landed them in prison. Of course, Prison Fellowship was about more than moral reform of inmates; it was about reaching them with the good news of Jesus Christ, which provides a moral standard and, more importantly, a Savior.

Chuck intended to write this book himself. He poured his soul into writing and producing the film series and knew this material inside and out. At one point just prior to the start of filming, he told me he was surprised at how much work and how complicated it was to produce a film, to which I replied, "Now you know why Hollywood producers get paid so much!" But Chuck went home to be with the Lord in the spring of 2012 before he could even begin writing the book that he wanted to accompany the film. I am delighted and honored to have been asked by the Colson Center and Zondervan to complete what was only on the drawing board when Chuck died. I was personally involved in the film series, as a panelist in episodes 4 and 5, and have had access to the various drafts of the script. In addition, I was a speaker/panelist at many of the launch conferences that accompanied the release of the film series in half a dozen major US cities. It was during these conferences and especially during the downtime that I was able to spend time with Chuck and hear his heart for a revival of ethics in our culture.

You may be wondering, *Why should I read this book if I've seen the film series?* or *If I've read the book, should I see the film series?* Both are fair questions. As with any movie, reading the book on which it is based adds a lot, because the movie can't possibly include everything in the book. Moreover the book adds details and precision that are difficult to bring out in the film. In this case, the book is actually based on the movie and develops in more detail things that, due to the constraints of time, we could barely touch on in the film or couldn't touch on at all.

The film series was intended to appeal to as broad an audience as possible. Chuck wanted the film to be used in state universities, companies, hospitals, and business schools, and not just to appeal to those with a Christian worldview. As a result, the film series does not make explicit the biblical and theological assumptions of Chuck and all the panelists. In fact, the film took some criticism for not being "biblical enough." Chuck anticipated that criticism and was okay with the trade-off that made the film more appealing to the secular organizations that he very much wanted to use the film. The film series took what is known as a *natural law* approach, which emphasizes the moral values God has made known *outside* the pages of the Bible. I explain that approach more in chapter 2. In the book, however, I draw out some of the biblical and theological assumptions that make up ethics within a Christian worldview.

I encourage you to see the film series after you finish the book. As is usually the case when you see a movie after reading the book it is based on, you will have a better understanding of the film series and will appreciate it more. Moreover, the visual experience of the film will draw you in and have an emotional impact on you. I suggest that you show the film series in your church, your school, your company, or even in your neighborhood. It is ideally suited to settings where not everyone shares a Christian worldview. Having read the book will make you a better discussion leader for those times when you show the film yourself.

The book follows the film series for all the chapters. Chapter 1 answers the question "How did we get into this ethical mess?" We will begin with the collapse of the financial system that caused the economic meltdown, the effects of which we are still experiencing today. And we will see that ethical failures occurred at virtually every stage of the economic crisis. We will uncover further evidence of moral decay in the culture and see the incoherence of many views of morality that are popular today and contrast that incoherence with what ethics in a Christian worldview looks like.

Chapters 2 and 3 bring out the foundational ideas of the book. In chapter 2 I ask and answer the question "Is there a moral law that we can know and live by?" I will defend the idea that all human beings have an innate moral sense, the law "written on the heart." I will affirm that morality is a matter of truth and can be known, and is not just a matter of opinion. We will discover an important distinction between objective and subjective truth as it relates to morality. We are moral beings by virtue of being made in God's image, not because morality evolved and is in our genes or in our brain. We will see that morality needs belief in God in order to be coherent and adequately grounded.

Chapter 3 asks and answers an equally important question: "If we know what is right, can we do it?" This is the area of moral psychology and deals with our moral inclinations, both for ourselves personally and for our culture. We will look at virtue within a distinctively Christian worldview and ask ourselves, "Can a person become virtuous apart from a relationship with Christ?" Or to put it another way, can someone cultivate virtue apart from spiritual renewal? We will look at this from the perspective of the apostle Paul in Romans 6 – 8, which suggests that often there is an inverse relationship between what we know and what we are inclined to do.

Chapters 4 through 6 discuss the application of these fundamental aspects of ethics to specific areas of life. Chapter 4 looks at ethics in medicine and health care and focuses on protecting the fundamental and intrinsic dignity of all human beings, regardless of their illnesses or impairments. Chapter 5 looks at ethics in the marketplace and makes the case that virtue is necessary for a properly functioning market economy and civil society. Chapter 6 deals with ethics in government and public life.

Our goal for both the book and film series is to help you think clearly and biblically about ethics, a subject of crucial significance in cultures all over the world today, and to contribute to a "reformation of manners" in your sphere of influence. But we also hope this book touches you personally and encourages you to cultivate virtue in your life and to nurture virtue in the next generation.

The survival of civil society and a flourishing market economy depend on the maintenance of virtue. As the French existentialist philosopher Albert Camus put it, "A man without ethics is a wild beast loosed upon the world."

CHAPTER 1

We're in an Ethical Mess!

One of evangelical Christian leader Chuck Colson's favorite ways to start a conversation about ethics was to ask someone, "What do you think caused the financial crisis?" He was, of course, referring to the meltdown of the US financial system that began in 2008 and caused a worldwide recession worse than any since the Great Depression of the 1920s and '30s. The effects of this recession are still with us today in the lost jobs, foreclosed homes, and large number of people who have either given up trying to find work or are underemployed.

What do *you* think caused the financial crisis? Think about that question for a minute. How would you have answered Chuck? My guess is that whatever your answer, it will have something to do with ethics — specifically, the collapse of ethics.

Let's look a bit more closely at the financial crisis and the various players in it and what happened to each of them. The financial meltdown centered on the home mortgage industry but infected the entire financial system, coming within a few days of bringing it to a collapse. The following chart will help us see what took place.

BORROWERS	LENDERS	PACKAGERS	ASSESSORS
Home owners	Mortgage brokers	Banks/Wall St./ Fannie Mae/ Freddie Mac	Ratings agencies

INVESTORS	INSURERS	POLICY MAKERS
Pensions, hedge funds, international institutions	Credit default swaps	Government, Federal Reserve

Here, in a very simplified way, is how the collapse occurred. Borrowers took out home loans from lenders, or mortgage brokers, who usually sold the loans to the packagers, the banks — mainly those on Wall Street — but also to what are called "government-sponsored entities" (GSEs) that go by the abbreviations Fannie Mae and Freddie Mac. These organizations would buy most mortgage loans and package them into investments. The interest borrowers paid on these mortgages was the income the investors were interested in. Remember, in the early 2000s when this started, the stock market was very volatile, having just come out of the dot.com crash and the economic problems created by the 9/11 terrorist attacks. As a result, the Federal Reserve kept interest rates very low, and they are still very low today. That's why you can't earn much more than 1 percent interest on most savings accounts today. Investors were understandably nervous about the roller-coaster ride the stock market had become, and investing in bonds that had very low interest rates was not attractive, so they were looking for other investments that were more secure than stocks but paid more than most bonds.

The banks were buying up mortgage loans that paid 5 to 7 percent interest and repackaging them into investment securities they sold to investors. The packagers would bundle together thousands of mortgages and sell them off in pieces to investors who were eager to have high returns without the volatility of the stock market. The ratings agencies gave these investments (called "mortgage-backed securities," or MBS) their highest ratings (AAA), which assured investors they were safe. The mortgage brokers, banks, and ratings agencies were paid handsome fees for their roles in this pipeline, and everyone was happy with the huge sums of money being made.

Even the insurance companies got into the act, because the risk to the investors was that the borrowers would default on their loans, thus making the investment securities based on those mortgages less valuable. If enough of them defaulted, the security would be worthless, because only a trickle of interest would be paid to the investors. So insurance companies like AIG sold what are called "credit default swaps," which is a fancy term for an insurance policy that protects the investors should the borrowers default or refinance their loans. It seemed like the system was a win for everyone. So what went wrong?

At every step, something went wrong — and went wrong ethically. Borrowers borrowed more than they could repay, many knowing they wouldn't be able to repay and would simply walk away from their homes. Mortgage brokers became less and less concerned with how credit-worthy borrowers were since they were going to sell the loans they made to the banks. They got paid whether or not the borrowers made good on their loans. They initiated what came to be called "liars loans" or "NINJA loans," which stood for "no income, no job or assets." These mortgage brokers often manipulated borrowers into loans they couldn't afford. The banks were selling mortgage-backed securities they knew were worthless to investors, and increasingly they would bet against the securities they were selling to investors (referred to as "selling them short"). The ratings agencies blessed these mortgage-backed securities with their highest ratings because they were being paid by the banks to issue their ratings (putting them into a major conflict of interest). Government played its role too, by putting Fannie and Freddie into a conflicted position — they could essentially buy off their regulators with campaign contributions, for which they became well known. In addition, the government pressured the lenders to increase home ownership to minority communities (the Community Reinvestment Act), causing them to make loans to less-credit-worthy borrowers. And the Federal Reserve kept interest rates very low for some time, encouraging people to amass a debt load they couldn't carry.

Actor and economist Ben Stein had this to say about what caused the financial meltdown:

> Well, the crash really started in 2007. And actually, it started even before that, when there was a law passed, and then repeatedly amended in the later part of the twentieth century, called the Community Reinvestment Act, which greatly encouraged lenders to lend to less-credit-worthy buyers. Lenders were encouraged, both emotionally and also in terms of finance, by the government to do that. So lenders started lending to a great, great many people who were not really credit-worthy.... This became a really, really big business, because people on Wall Street saw that, first of all, there was hardly any government supervision of it. What they saw was that they could take large bundles of mortgages. They sold them to fiduciary institutions, especially pension funds. At the same time, they sold them short. They sold them short and hammered them like mad by buying credit-default-swap insurance, which is a giant short instrument. And then they basically raked in money. And then, at the bottom of the cycle, they bought the bonds back and made money on that part of the cycle. At every level, they were deceiving the people they were dealing with. At every level.... *At the heart of this is an unethical series of acts.* At the heart of it was the incredibly unethical act of Wall Street in packaging securities they knew to be fragile and often worthless, or largely worthless. They shouldn't have sold them in the first place. If they were selling them, they should not, at the same time, have been selling them short.... In a sense, there was an ethical issue with the public as well, because the public, to be sure goaded by the

mortgage brokers, was taking on debt that they couldn't repay, and it is not ethical to take on a debt that you can't repay. Yes, you should not be suckered into it by unscrupulous loan brokers. But, if you borrow money, you should have it in your heart that you're going to repay it.[1]

When it came to holding people and institutions responsible for the financial debacle and the ethical failures that caused it, there was quite a bit of reluctance to assign responsibility. Longtime Wall Street observer Jim Grant (*Grant's Interest Rate Observer*) put it this way: "You know, in the aftermath of the bust, in the dark days of 2008 and early 2009, you'd hear our public officials say, over and over, 'Let's not have any recriminations. Let's not point fingers and blame.' Without accountability, we are all treading water in this murky, lukewarm, milky sea of collectivism, and nothing good comes of it. Let us have individual responsibility."

EVIDENCE OF MORAL DECLINE

Of course, Wall Street is not the only example of moral decline, only the most recent. Evidence of moral decay in our culture is all around us. Education experts tell us there is an epidemic of cheating in schools today, and many educators feel powerless to stop it.[2] In some cases, in order to meet state standards, some teachers and administrators have actually helped students cheat by providing advance copies of the tests. You can say much the same thing about truth telling, another casualty of the moral decline in the culture. Lying is much more common than a generation ago, and some of the most high-profile legal cases have revolved around the cover-ups more than the alleged crime. *Wall Street Journal* writer James Stewart, in his book on lying under oath, commented, "Mounting evidence suggests that the broad public commitment to telling the truth under oath has been breaking down, a trend that has been accelerating in recent years."[3] And that's just the evidence from people who are *under oath* to tell the truth! That doesn't even begin to capture the erosion of truth telling in business and private life. Most of the well-publicized business scandals of the last decade (Enron, WorldCom, Arthur Andersen, and many other companies in accounting scandals) are essentially cases of accounting and financial reporting fraud. Not to mention the outrageously extreme case of Bernie Madoff, the investment adviser who swindled clients out of roughly $65 billion.

Along with cheating and lying comes theft. Shoplifting, or retail stealing, has also reached epidemic proportions. An entire industry has been built around retailers' need for loss prevention and security, and the FBI estimates theft costs retailers roughly $30 billion per year.

Another example of moral decline is rampant drug use, leading more influential leaders to admit the war on drugs is a failure and to push for legalization of some drugs. And it is not just the abuse of traditional drugs that is on the rise — it is also the abuse of prescription drugs, especially various kinds of painkillers.

Pornography is everywhere today and available at the click of a mouse. In fact, the majority of Internet traffic is by porn users. With this has come the particularly pernicious sexualization of young girls in the media and in advertising.[4] Not surprisingly, the increases in sexual assault and sexual abuse of children continue to be alarming. Around the world, we have seen dramatic increases in human trafficking and sexual slavery, and in some countries in the developing world, pedophilia is a legal and widespread practice.

The traditional family continues to come unraveled, and the number of households with a mom and a dad living under the same roof is now a minority. Increasingly, kids are having kids, and today we give baby showers to teenagers who are pregnant, as though that were a cause for celebration. The fraying of families increasingly produces children and young adults whose moral compasses are damaged, giving them a skewed view of morality.

Perhaps the most dramatic evidence of moral decline in the culture comes from the rise of the prison population. As Chuck Colson reported, when he began working in the prison system with Prison Fellowship in the late 1970s, there were 229,000 inmates in US prisons. Today there are 2.3 million, a tenfold increase. Colson summarized the moral landscape in America like this: "It's an inescapable consequence of neglecting moral training. We're in an ethical mess because of it. We're all paying the price, and we're all pointing fingers at other people when the real problem is all of us aren't addressing the need for *character formation* in our lives. That's at the heart of the breakdown that we're seeing in American life today."

Sociologist James Davison Hunter, in his book *The Death of Character*, amplifies the ethical disarray of the culture, describing the deeper problem:

> We say we want a renewal of character in our day, but we don't really know what we ask for. To have a renewal of character is to have a renewal of a creedal order that constrains, limits, binds, obligates, and compels. This price is too high for us to pay (as a culture). We want character without unyielding conviction; we want strong morality but without the emotional burden of guilt and shame; we want virtue but without particular moral justifications that invariably offend; we want good without having to name evil; we want decency without the authority to insist on it; we want moral community without any limitations to personal freedom. *In short, we want what we cannot possibly have on the terms that we want it.*[5]

THE INCOHERENCE OF RELATIVISM

Part of the reason we're in an ethical mess is because of the way people *think* about morality. Whenever someone makes a comment about something being right or wrong, it's very interesting to ask them, "Where do right and wrong come from?" This will often reveal a sense of incoherence in the way they think about ethics. Princeton professor Robert George describes this confusion about morality:

> On the one hand, people believe that there are some things that are just plain wrong: murder, rape, theft, and deception.

> But on the other hand, the polling data makes very clear that many, many Americans, at some level, at least claim to believe in what's called *moral relativism*: the denial that there is any such thing as moral truth, or an objective moral truth, that all we have is opinion. There are no right and wrong answers to moral questions, just opinions or feelings.

We seem to want it both ways when we think about morality — we believe some things are obviously and absolutely wrong, like slavery and sexual assault, but we also want to believe that morality is relative, a matter of opinion. I will take up this idea of morality being a matter of fact or opinion in chapter 2. For now, let's see where people commonly think ethics come from. The incoherence in our thinking about ethics that Professor George describes is expressed in many different ways in today's culture. Here are a few:

"What gives you the right to judge?"

My good friend and Baylor University philosophy professor Frank Beckwith describes being confronted with this question when he participated in a debate on abortion at a major university. He commented that he believed abortion was morally wrong in most cases. He was immediately attacked by one of the panelists with the question (which wasn't really a question but a statement), "What gives you the right to judge?" He answered it in a way that his fellow panelist didn't quite expect. He said, "Well, I think I'm very qualified to judge. I have a master's and a doctorate in this field, I've written several books on the subject, lectured on it around the world, and have generally given it a great deal of careful thought." His opponent was not particularly impressed with his qualifications but didn't know quite what to say in response, except to make it clear that her point in asking the question was to say that no one had a right to make these particular moral judgments. What was so interesting about this exchange was that she was making a moral judgment on Frank for being narrow-minded and judgmental, while at the same time insisting that no one had the right to make these kinds of judgments! When people say, "What gives you the right to judge?" they really mean that no one should make a moral judgment on another person. The incoherence of saying that no one has the right to make moral judgments becomes obvious when anyone tries to live out the statement. Usually they give up this view when they are the victim of an injustice — then they become not only willing to judge but insistent on making a judgment that they have been wronged.

Follow your own conscience.

This is what I call the "Jiminy Cricket" view of morality — let your conscience be your guide. If you remember the Disney movie *Pinocchio* you saw as a child, you'll remember that before Pinocchio goes out to face the world, his friend Jiminy Cricket advises him to let his conscience be his guide. Ironically, after receiving that advice, Pinocchio gets into all sorts of trouble, suggesting that his conscience wasn't such a great guide after all. Michael Miller of the Acton Institute responded to this advice to follow your own conscience like this: "In business school, when we had discussions on ethics, they said, 'What's ethics?' They said well, 'Ethics is following your own integrity, or following your conscience.' *But what if you have a poorly formed conscience? What if you're a jerk?*" Or to take it further, what if you have no conscience at all, as is the case with sociopaths, who feel no guilt or remorse when committing heinous crimes? This view is also incoherent, because a person following his or her conscience may do just fine until their conscience allows for an injustice against someone else. If you are that person who has been wronged, you tend to give up your view that people should follow their conscience pretty quickly.

Values are what you value.

This is a very subjective view of morality (I take up the distinction between objective and subjective views of morality more in chapter 2) and another expression of moral relativism. History professor Glenn Sunshine talks about what happened when his daughter was taught this view of where morals come from by a high school teacher. He says, "My daughter Elizabeth was in high school at one point, and she had a class on, well I suppose it would be the closest they would have to ethics. They said the definition of the word 'values' is whatever it is that you value. That's what values are, whatever you value. So she came home and said, 'Okay, Dad, so if I value good grades better than I value honesty, it's okay for me to cheat?' She got it immediately. It's incoherent."

We make up our own moral rules for ourselves.

This is a very common way of expressing moral relativism. Either cultures make their own moral rules (cultural relativism) or individuals make up their own moral rules for themselves (individual relativism or moral subjectivism) where morality is determined by their own tastes and preferences. You may hear of this practice when sexual morality is discussed or in matters of marriage and family. I heard of it when I was speaking on morality and ethics to a group of public high school students some time ago. I asked where their view of right and wrong came from, and a handful of students expressed versions of "We make up our own moral rules for ourselves." One of the students in the front row had a brand-new iPhone on her desk. I walked over to her desk, picked up the phone, and casually put it in my pocket, all the while continuing with my talk. She grew more and more concerned as the session came to a close, and she finally said, "Aren't you going to give me my phone back?" I calmly replied, "No, I'm not." When she started to protest, I cut her off by saying, "But I thought you said that we all make up our own moral rules for ourselves. My moral rules are that adults who are older and wiser are entitled to the stuff of students who are younger and inexperienced in life." She didn't know quite what to say, so she blurted out, "But that's wrong; that's not fair." I then pointed out to her the incoherency of her views of morality and how quickly she abandoned her relativism and became a moral absolutist when an injustice was done to her. She recognized that some things, like stealing someone's phone, are just plain wrong. You can't have it both ways — claim that we make up our own moral rules for ourselves and then give up your relativism when you need a moral absolute, as you do when confronting injustice.

My friend Dr. Beckwith, whom I mentioned earlier, created a teachable moment for one of his students in pointing out the incoherency of these views of morality. The student submitted a philosophy paper defending moral relativism. It was very well done and clearly deserved an A grade. The professor wrote at the end of the paper, "Great paper, well argued, clear and cogent. Grade — F." The student, predictably, went ballistic when he got his paper back, claiming that he was unfairly graded. Of course, he was appealing to the overriding moral value of fairness, at which point his professor indicated that he was actually giving up the view he had defended in his paper!

Chuck Colson talked about the incoherency of relativism when he gave a provocative lecture on ethics at Harvard Business School. He said:

> Twenty years ago, a friend of mine gave $5 million to Harvard Business School to set up a chair on ethics. I called him and said, "You're wasting your money, because an institution, today, committed to philosophical relativism, can't possibly teach ethics. Ethics are based on absolute standards of right and wrong." So I wrote an article about it after he told me that he thought I was wrong. It got a lot of publicity. As a matter of fact, I got a lot of flak from friends of mine at Harvard. I ended up getting invited to give a distinguished lecture at the Harvard Business School entitled "Why Harvard Can't Teach Ethics," and the room was packed — students, faculty, 350 of them. I prepared harder for that than any talk I've given in years, because I knew I was going to be assaulted by the best and the brightest. When I got all through a forty-five-minute talk and opened it up for questions, there wasn't one good question. The students simply were not aware of questions of moral philosophy. It was a very disappointing experience for me because

there was just no engagement. I found the same thing at Yale and my own alma mater, Brown University.[6]

Colson argued that what passed for ethics education at Harvard Business School was pragmatism and that was good for business—but not ethics. He maintained that ethics depends on standards that are more than simply human creations, standards that transcend time and culture.[7]

Or you can hear about the incoherency of relativism from a graduate of Harvard Business School. Donovan Campbell explained the incoherence in the view of morality he received there. It was quite a contrast to his background in the Marine Corps. He explained:

> I'm a graduate of Harvard Business School. I graduated with high distinction. I was named a Baker Scholar. So I was in the top 5 percent of the class. There were two leadership classes: one of which specifically focused on the responsibility of business leaders in the context of business; the other on the ethics of business and the moral context of business. And what made that class difficult is that, unlike in the Marine Corps, everyone comes in and Harvard doesn't tell them, "All right. Here's the deal. Here's right and here's wrong. There's a common set of ground rules that you all just need to subscribe to. And if you don't subscribe to that, you're just wrong." Because, unfortunately, the school does not subscribe to the idea of ultimate morality, of ultimate good, which is good in and of itself, outside of any context and which is translatable across cultures, times, it's applicable everywhere. They do not subscribe to that concept. So there might be some who make the argument, with some justification, that if the context of a culture is bribery, and that is what is culturally acceptable, and that is the way that local business is done, then there is a very compelling case for a First-World company to come in and bribe. The problem is there's no mandate. *There's no fundamental*

agreement on the way the world works. And so you're
reduced to discussing practical behavior in certain situations.

Either morality is a human creation or it comes from a transcendent source beyond the boundaries of this world. In other words, morality is either created or discovered. For most of the history of the West, from classical times until today, it has been held that morality is discerned, not created by human beings. In America, until the 1960s we lived off the Judeo-Christian moral system that was at the heart of the Founding Fathers' view of civil society. For some time, even though the society at large had rejected the Christian worldview more generally, its moral consensus held considerable influence on the moral views people held and the way they talked about morality. Since the 1960s, that moral consensus has come unraveled, leaving the culture with a mixture of incoherent views of morality, of which relativism is at the top of the list.[8]

Ethics in a Christian Worldview

In the film series Doing the Right Thing, the producers were aiming to tell the story of ethics and have it appeal to as wide an audience as possible. Doing that involved an approach that did not necessarily make explicit the Christian foundations for ethics but relied mostly on reason and common sense about morality. Part of the task of the companion book is to make clear the theological fundamentals for ethics. In other words, what might a distinctively Christian ethic look like?

In contrast to the rampant relativism of our day, Christian ethics holds out a coherent view of morality. Christian ethics insists that there is such a thing as right and wrong, good and evil, and is unafraid to call evil what it is, as unfashionable as that has become today. If someone calls something evil today, he or she is widely presumed to be judgmental, unenlightened, or a cultural imperialist (a person who believes his or her culture is morally superior to all others). However, Christian ethics fits well with our basic moral intuitions that some things are simply and unequivocally evil, such as genocide, racial prejudice, the murder of innocent people, and sexual assault.

As opposed to morality being strictly a human creation, ethics within a Christian worldview comes from a *transcendent* source, namely God, specifically his character and commands. Another way to put this is that Christian ethics consists of both virtues and values based ultimately on God's character. That is, the virtues are primary, since the ultimate basis for morality is God's character, and moral values follow from God's character traits. Think of it this way: the reason God commands that we love one another is not mainly because love makes the world go round, though it does. The main reason God commands that we love one another is that God is a loving, compassionate being. Love for one another is a moral value because it is fundamentally a part of who God is. Similarly, God commands that we be forgiving people, not mainly because forgiveness heals fractured relationships, though it does. Rather, it's because God is fundamentally a forgiving God.

We see that God's character is foundational to ethics when we consider what ethics might look like if God's commands were the primary component. If morality were determined by God's commands, then *whatever* God commanded would be right, and whatever he prohibited would be wrong. But that would mean God could command anything he so desired, and simply by doing so that would make it right. But we know that's not true — there are some things God could not command. For example, God could not command that we torture babies for fun and profit. The reason we know that is because a loving God would not command any such thing! But as soon as we make that statement, we are admitting that God's commands are not the ultimate basis for morality — his character, that of being a loving God, is. What he can command is limited by his character.[9]

In contrast to the moral subjectivity of the culture — we make up our own moral rules for ourselves, and they are determined by how we feel about them — Christian ethics are *objective*. That is, the validity of any segment of a Christian ethic is independent of how someone feels about it, whether it is well received or not. For example, sexual ethics in the culture are largely determined by the notion of "if it feels right, then it must be right." This is why it is widely held in the culture that a diversity of opposing positions can all be right — homosexuality is right for the gay person, heterosexuality is right for the straight person, and bisexuality is right for the bisexual person. By contrast, Christian ethics are objective — they are true regardless of how someone feels about them. I will look at this distinction between objective and subjective truth in more detail in chapter 2. Suffice it to say for now that a morality based on God's character and commands is objectively true, and such a morality is a fact, not an opinion. For example, if someone believes that murdering innocent people is morally acceptable, that is not just a difference of opinion. Anyone who believes it is okay to murder the innocent is wrong, because murdering innocents is one of those things that is just plain wrong. Similarly, as my colleague William Lane Craig says, "Anyone who believes that sexual assault is okay needs therapy, not an argument!"[10]

However, just because morality is objective doesn't mean everyone agrees about everything in ethics. No, there is widespread disagreement on topics about which it may be more difficult to discern what morality demands. We may disagree on what God commands or on how to apply the more general principles of Christian ethics. That's where experience, debate, and deliberation come in as the means to clarify what ethics demands of us. Remember, we human beings are very skilled at rationalization and self-deception, and it may be that in many cases we actually know the right thing to do but don't want to be subject to objective, transcendent moral demands. We don't want someone, namely God, telling us how to live our lives. But if God exists and has spoken about morality, then ethics are both transcendent and objective.

In a diverse culture, moral disagreement should not be a surprise. In the Christian worldview, the fact that the world is broken due to sin accounts for moral disparities. But if morality is not objective, then moral disagreements are settled by appeals to power—and that makes the world a very dangerous place. Ask people who have lived under authoritarian governments that enforce morality based on power. By contrast, in a properly functioning democracy, you can have moral disagreement without having to worry about someone tyrannizing another. Morality becomes clear and is enforced as consensus emerges, as was the case with slavery and civil rights, but not so much with abortion, on which no consensus currently exists, though consensus by itself is a recognition of morality not a determinant of it. The law usually reflects an underlying moral consensus, though today we see more frequent bypassing of debate and deliberation in favor of simply trying to change the law.

Not only are Christian ethics transcendent and objective, they are also *universal*—that is, they are not confined to any particular culture or group. Things are right or wrong independent of the culture you're in. For example, murdering innocents is wrong regardless of the culture you happen to be in. Sexual assault is wrong whether you're in the West or the Middle East. Racial discrimination is wrong everywhere it's practiced. Just because something is culturally accepted does not necessarily make it right. In parts of the Middle East, women have very few rights to live their lives as they choose. In Nazi Germany, discrimination against Jews, culminating in genocide, enjoyed fairly wide cultural acceptance. But just because the culture accepts something does not necessarily make it right, because morality is universal, transcending time and culture, though the application of moral values and virtues may look different in different cultures. A good bit of what passes for moral diversity is a difference in application of moral values that cultures hold in common. For example, simply because we live in another time period does not mean the demands of morality necessarily change. Slavery is just as wrong today as it was hundreds of years ago. Adultery is just as wrong today as when the Ten Commandments prohibited it. The application of moral principles may change as time changes—we would expect that they would. So what justice or fairness look like today in an information age economy would be different than what it looked like during the time the Bible was written, in a largely agricultural economy.

Finally, Christian ethics are *knowable*. That is, they can be known, though they are known differently than what we can know with our senses. Morality is a matter of knowledge, not opinion or belief. But most people in the culture believe that morality is a matter of taste, preference, or opinion, and that the real stuff we can know is what we can empirically verify. Professor Glenn Sunshine says this of the cultural change that occurred:

> The key to this is to understand that a few centuries ago we had an integrated vision of life, where morality, the physical world, ethics, metaphysics ... all of these things were wrapped up into a single, coherent package. Then there was a shift in the culture, where there was a growing emphasis on the material world being the world of objective fact, objective knowledge, and everything else got pushed aside into the realm of opinion or faith. Now, this worked okay for a while, because we were living on what some theologians call "borrowed capital." The fact is that the Christian ethical foundations of Western civilization continued to have an influence in shaping our culture's values and behavior. That can only last so long, though, when there's no foundation left for it. So what's happened is that, over time, the Christian moral foundations that allow you to make the kinds of ethical and moral judgments that you're talking about here have deteriorated. So that they're still exerting some sort of influence on the society, so that we still say things are right and wrong, but, increasingly, *our behavior is lining up more with the underlying belief that the material world is all that's really real, and that everything else is just a matter of opinion.*

Professor Sunshine makes a very important observation that I develop more in chapter 2 — that morality (and religion) has been relegated to the realm of belief and therefore cannot be either true or false. What this does to morality is to make it unknowable and therefore only a matter of faith. I suspect that this view of morality has crept into many Christian contexts and, in doing so, has caused many people who claim to follow Jesus and adhere to a Christian ethic to adopt the same incoherent view of morality that is widespread in the culture.

The Bible is very clear that people are accountable to the demands of morality precisely because they can know them. God has revealed his moral values and virtues both in his Word, the Bible, and in his world, what we refer to as "natural law." That is, God revealed his moral values outside the pages of the Bible. Romans 2:14–16 refers to this as the law written on our hearts, suggesting that even if someone did not have access to the Bible, he or she was still accountable to the demands of morality. For example, adultery is just as wrong for someone who does not have access to the Bible as it is for the Christian who does. The same holds for murder, theft, lying, and other moral mandates. University of Texas professor J. Budziszewski calls this concept "what we can't not know."[11] In other words, God has made his moral demands clear both in his Word and in his world. A clear example of this sense of natural law in the Bible occurs in what are called "the oracles to the nations." These are parts of the Old Testament books of the prophets in which the prophets announce judgment both against Israel and against the surrounding nations for many of the same things — violence, oppression of the poor, injustice, and idolatry (worshiping false gods) — for which Israel was guilty. And remember: the nations did not have access to God's law, yet they were still held accountable for upholding a standard of morality God had revealed via natural law.

What all of this suggests is that everyone, by virtue of being made in God's image, has an innate moral sense, though it may have been corrupted somewhat by sin. This helps explain the tremendous moral similarities among cultures. We often highlight our moral diversity and forget the similarities among various cultures. But virtually all cultures have prohibitions on taking innocent life, lying, theft, and sex outside prescribed boundaries (such as adultery and incest). In fact, C. S. Lewis cataloged much of this moral similarity in his book *The Abolition of Man*.[12] Whereas the relativism of the culture highlights our moral differences, natural law highlights our moral similarities. It is true that we do have moral differences, but a Christian worldview accounts for this well with its view of original sin — which has clouded the lenses through which fallen human beings perceive natural law. But natural law also accounts for our moral similarities.

I learned a good lesson in natural law from, of all places, the public schools. When my kids were younger, I would volunteer to help out in their elementary school classrooms from time to time. During one of those times, when I walked into the classroom, I noticed there were dozens of moral maxims displayed all around the room. They included things like "Play fair," "Don't cheat," "Be kind," "Show respect," "Be compassionate," "Be forgiving," and "Don't be mean." I soon realized this was part of a larger school program to highlight particular character traits the teachers wanted to encourage in the students. I wondered, *Who decided that these maxims and traits would be the ones they would emphasize?* and *How did they come up with these?* It soon occurred to me that the teachers recognized these as almost self-evident, and I realized that the reason they recognized them as such was not a coincidence or an accident. It was the result of God's revelation outside the Bible — otherwise known as natural law. What this indicates is that although there is moral disagreement, there is still a reservoir of shared values and virtues we recognize as important to communicate to the next generation of students in the public schools. This further illustrates the moral incoherence I have mentioned so often in this chapter — claiming to be relativists who make up our moral rules for ourselves and, at the same time, acknowledging some universal and objective values, such as the ones on the walls of my son's elementary school classroom.

CONCLUSION

Psychiatrist Stan Samenow conducted a seventeen-year longitudinal study of prisoners in the prison system, trying to discover what factors led to someone ending up in prison. He anticipated that those factors would be things like poverty, lack of education, broken family background, or lack of job opportunities. But instead, he found that in the vast majority of cases, men and women ended up in prison because of *making wrong moral decisions*. Dr. Samenow highlighted the importance of ethics and making right moral decisions. This is critical to a society in which freedom is paramount. Free societies cannot survive without ethics and virtue. Our country's Founding Fathers never envisioned that a free society could function without what they called "civic virtue." They assumed that a virtuous people were best suited for self-government, and they saw that the American experiment in democracy could not flourish apart from a moral (and religious) people. This is why people committed to "doing the right thing" are crucial for society to remain free.

CHAPTER 2

Is There a
Moral Law
We Can Know?

One of the most important documents of the twentieth century was written on scraps of toilet paper from a prison cell in Birmingham, Alabama. When Martin Luther King Jr. wrote his now well-known "Letter from a Birmingham Jail" in 1963, it galvanized the civil rights movement and pricked the conscience of America. Today it is assigned reading for high school students so that they might understand African-Americans' struggle for civil rights in this country. In the letter, King articulated a principled, objective, and transcendent moral basis for standing up against one of the greatest moral evils of his time — racial discrimination and segregation. If you read the letter carefully, you will find that King used a good deal of biblical imagery, especially from the Old Testament prophets' condemnation of those who perpetuated injustice by oppressing the vulnerable. Yet he clearly expected all people to accept the fundamental principle of racial equality whether or not they respected the Bible. Princeton professor Robert George says:

It's that principle of equality, the equal worth of every human being, no matter how high or how low in the world's eyes, no matter how rich or poor, weak or strong. That's the principle to which Dr. King appealed. Now, the question is, where did he get it? He got it out of this basic tenet that comes in the very beginning of the Bible, and that is the proposition that man, though made from the dust of the earth, is nevertheless fashioned in the very image and likeness of God; the very image and likeness of the divine creator and ruler of the universe. That's where King got that fundamental notion. Now, does that notion depend on divine revelation? I would join King in saying "not necessarily."

I understood this better when helping my son with a school assignment. When my middle son, Cameron, was in high school, he was required to read King's letter and write an analysis of it for his English class. When I heard he was doing this assignment, I mentioned to him how King was a Christian, a pastor, and how he used the Bible's imagery to make his point. I encouraged him to look for the theological and biblical references in the letter. But after he read the excerpt his teacher had distributed to the class, he came to me puzzled and said, "Dad, what are you talking about? There's nothing theological in the letter!" I read over the passage he had read and couldn't find the biblical references either. So he looked up the letter in another source and read the entire piece, not just the sample his teacher had given out. When he finished reading it, he was angry with his teacher for omitting all of the theological references that were in the original version. He felt that his teacher was trivializing the theological foundation for King's views on civil rights.

But apart from the view of religion his teacher may have held, the assignment was still valuable. His teacher did not think the explicitly theological material was necessary to make King's main point about equal rights. King's letter was still very compelling, even as edited by his teacher. It was clearly grounded in his theology, but making that explicit was not necessary to make his point persuasive. Chuck Colson explained the point: "I think King proves more than anything else that there is a truth which is knowable.... It really is something we know, and this was what King was appealing to. He was appealing to this transcendent moral authority, which not only is there objectively, because every society has understood it, but is there subjectively because we know it internally."

In appealing to American society to do the right thing when it came to racial discrimination, King was assuming there is a right thing. That is, he was assuming there is a transcendent, objective, and universal moral law that can be known by all people regardless of their worldview. As his niece Alveda King put it:

> During my uncle's lifetime, when he had to consider whether he would obey the law or disobey the law, he had to think about the moral value of a law. When he was challenged by his critics, they would say, "King, you're stirring up strife. You're causing problems. You're breaking the law. You're bound to honor the law." My uncle did say, if a law is unjust, it is our moral responsibility to resist the unjust law. That is the basis of the civil rights movement.

King held that there is a transcendent moral law above the law of the land, and if the law of the land is unjust, the higher law is a priority. Ironically, King is celebrated almost universally as one of the greatest moral reformers of his century for his civil rights leadership. Yet a culture committed to moral relativism, as described in chapter 1, can't have a moral reformer like King, since that means challenging the moral status quo. Remember, for the cultural relativist, the moral consensus of the culture determines our ethics. If that's true, then any moral reformer is acting unethically! That's further evidence of our culture's incoherent view of morality — celebrating a moral reformer like Dr. King and claiming to be relativists at the same time. All great moral reformers had to appeal to a transcendent, objective, and universal moral law that opposed the existing moral consensus of the culture. That's what Nelson Mandela did in overcoming apartheid in South Africa.

That's what William Wilberforce did in leading the fight to abolish slavery in the British Empire. That's what Abraham Lincoln appealed to in ending slavery in America. And that's what the next great moral reformer will do too, perhaps when it comes to ending abortion or human trafficking.

I had to answer this same question about a higher law and my obligation to follow it when I was asked by a criminal court judge about my views on the subject. I was in a jury pool, being considered for jury service in a murder trial. The judge looked at my juror questionnaire and saw that I was a professor, and when he asked me what I taught and I replied, "Ethics," about a hundred potential jurors in the room erupted in laughter, thinking there was no possible way I would be chosen. To my amazement, I was eventually chosen and later picked to be foreman of the jury! But before I was selected, the judge had one more question. He said, "I see you teach at a religious college. Do you think you can follow the law?" Initially, I had no idea where he was going with this question, and my puzzled look prompted a follow-up question. He asked, "Do you believe there's a higher law above the law of the land?" He was concerned that I might not follow the criminal law if I felt it violated the higher moral law. Now understanding the point of the question, I answered, "Your Honor, I actually do believe the law of God is higher than the law of the land, but I don't anticipate that the two will conflict in this case. So yes, I think I can follow the law."

TRUTH AND MORALITY

Dr. King believed there was such a thing as *moral truth* that everyone could know and to which everyone was accountable. Those who believed racial discrimination was morally acceptable did not just have a difference of opinion; they were wrong. Similarly, Nelson Mandela believed in moral truth — that those who held that apartheid was ethically appropriate were not simply holding another opinion; they were just plain wrong. Most people in our culture, however, see morality not as a matter of knowledge and truth, but as opinion or belief. So maybe we need to go back and explore this idea of truth further.

Truth is, to put it simply, *correspondence to reality.* Philosopher Neal Plantinga explained it this way:

> People sometimes wonder what truth is. Well, truth is a property of a claim. You say it's raining today, and if it is in fact raining, then your statement is true. It's a relation of a claim to reality, a right relation, and we can know it. We can know truth, and we can know falsehood. Obviously this is crucial to commerce, to education, to the courts, to ordinary life. There is real truth and real falsehood. We can know them except when we corrupt ourselves by self-deception or in some other way. And then of course things can get really skewed.

Plantinga is right about how important the notion of truth is to our everyday life. For example, we assume a concept of truth in most of our communication with others. Unless there are compelling reasons not to expect the truth, we generally count on the truth in most of our verbal and written communication. If we did not or could not have this anticipation, it would not be long until meaningful communication would no longer be possible.

To be more specific, we need to make a distinction between two different kinds of statements — *objective and subjective statements.* Objective statements involve a claim about the way things are, about the way the world works. By contrast, subjective statements constitute a claim about a person's desires and preferences. Another way to put the difference is that the objective statements concern facts we discover, whereas subjective statements concern the subject's tastes and preferences.

My friend and former student Sean McDowell uses a creative exercise to make this subjective-objective distinction clear to his students. He puts several statements up on the screen and asks the students to shout out either "ice cream" or "insulin" at the statement. The "ice cream" designation indicates a subjective statement, which resembles someone's preference for flavors of ice cream. By contrast, the "insulin" label suggests an objective statement, which is akin to the statement that insulin is necessary for the body to process sugars.

Categorize the following statements as "ice cream" or "insulin":

1. Coke tastes better than Pepsi.
2. Diet Coke has fewer calories than regular Coke.
3. Hawaii is the most beautiful vacation spot on the earth.
4. George Washington was the first president of the United States.
5. I can bench-press 250 pounds.
6. Action movies are more enjoyable than romances.
7. The earth is the center of the solar system.
8. Abortion, unless the mother's life is threatened, is wrong.
9. Racial discrimination is wrong.

Let's think about these statements a bit more. Statements 1, 3, and 6 are all subjective claims that are nothing more than someone's preferences. They are true *for that person* but could be false for someone else. My believing such a statement makes it true subjectively. In other words, these three statements are all matters of opinion or taste. To say that it is true for a person means only that it is a reflection of his or her likings. By contrast, statements 2, 4, 5, and 7 are all objective claims. Statement 2 is an objective and empirical claim, meaning that it can be verified or falsified by empirical evidence. In this case, a simple calorie test can tell us if it is true or not. Statement 4 is an objective, historical claim. Historical testimony can either verify or falsify this claim about who the first American president was. Statement 5 is actually an objective claim that we don't know the answer to — though by looking at me, you might consider it unlikely, making it an objective yet false claim. Statement 7 is an objective claim that is false though at one time was believed to be true.

The most interesting of these statements is number 8 — "Abortion, unless the mother's life is threatened, is wrong." Whether you answer "ice cream" or "insulin" on this one makes a very big difference in how you view morality. This statement is a moral statement, making a claim about right and wrong. I suspect most people in our culture would answer this one as "ice cream," indicating their belief that this moral claim is subjective, a matter of opinion. But this is actually an objective statement, and the correct response to this is "insulin." This is because *moral statements are facts, not opinions.* They reflect the way things ought to be, not simply the way I believe them to be or want them to be. Maybe the reason people would answer this as "ice cream" is because the culture is so divided on the morality of abortion — there is not societal consensus on this. That might make it seem like the statement on abortion is more a matter of opinion. Many moral questions that don't have consensus seem like this. But don't be fooled into thinking that all moral claims are like that, because they are not. Just because we have moral differences, it does not follow that all moral claims are subjective, on the level of preferences about ice cream.

So take statement 9, "Racial discrimination is wrong." This is a clearer example of a moral statement being objective, and the average person in our culture might actually answer this one "insulin." I suspect most people would say that if a member of the KKK believed racial discrimination was okay, we would say that person doesn't just have a different opinion or a different perspective on the issue; we would say the person is wrong and the statement that "racial discrimination is okay" is false. When we say, "Racial discrimination is wrong," that statement is right, or true, and thus constitutes knowledge. It comports with reality in the moral universe, or the way things ought to be.

Philosophers call moral statements like statements 8 and 9 *normative* statements, which give us moral norms of right behavior. But they also are claims to what is true morally or what we can know morally. To express it another way, we *know* that racial discrimination is wrong. This is what we mean when we say there is a moral law we can *know.* Moral statements are objective statements: they are either true or false, and they constitute knowledge. We come to know them differently than we come to know other kinds of objective truths. Morality is verified differently than empirical facts, historical facts, or even legal facts. Morality is verified in some cases by an emerging consensus — it took some time for a consensus to emerge about slavery and civil rights, though as a culture we did finally get there. Morality is also verified by tradition and experience of what makes for a flourishing society (the natural law tradition). And from a distinctly Christian worldview, morality is verified by God's character and by his statements in his Word about morality.

Let's take another example — the statement that "sexual assault is wrong." In the words of my colleague William Lane Craig as cited in chapter 1, anyone who disagrees with that statement needs therapy, not an argument! We seem to *know* that sexual assault is wrong, and someone (however rare such persons might be) who would make the case that sexual assault is morally okay does not simply have a different opinion but is simply wrong.

The problem with saying that morality is like ice cream is if that is true, then we can really have valid differences of opinion on the morality of things like racial discrimination and sexual assault, not to mention other moral areas, such as human trafficking, the murder of innocents, kidnapping, theft, honor killings, female circumcision, and many other areas in which we don't permit differences of views. What that means practically is that *if morality is like ice cream, then no one can ever make a moral judgment about anything.* That would be like judging people for their taste in ice cream! Yet, as I pointed out in chapter 1, no one can live as a consistent moral subjectivist, and people commonly give up their relativism when they are victims of a clear injustice. That is, when victims of injustice, people make moral statements that they expect to be taken as *objective* statements that constitute knowledge. They do not consider that people who think victimizing them is morally okay just have a difference of opinion. They consider them wrong, and interestingly, they consider themselves *to have been wronged.*

People sometimes have an intriguing way of defending the idea that morality is a subjective matter of opinion. For example, with the discussion of the morality of abortion, it is common to hear things like, "If you don't like abortion, then don't have one!" You can easily see how a statement like that reduces the moral claim that "abortion is wrong" to a strictly personal matter, thereby denying that it has any value as truth and knowledge, and further denying that the claim applies more broadly than just to yourself. Consider what it would be like to approach other moral claims that way. Imagine telling Dr. King, "If you don't like slavery, then don't own slaves!" I suspect he would have been incredulous at a statement like that. Whether someone owns slaves or has abortions or participates in human trafficking is irrelevant because the issue is so much bigger than you and your personal feelings about it. How you feel about these things is important, but your feelings do not determine what's right or wrong. This is precisely because moral statements are not fundamentally subjective truths. They are objective truths that constitute knowledge about the moral universe.

This discussion about objective and subjective morality is not merely an academic exercise but has significant cultural ramifications. If morality is viewed as subjective when it actually is objective, this erodes not only the concept of morality but also the ability of people to do what is right and stand for what is good. They will lack the courage to stand up for moral goodness in the face of evil. This is what C. S. Lewis lamented way back in the 1940s in his essay "Men without Chests," which appears as a chapter in his book *The Abolition of Man*.[1] He was critiquing the educational system in the United Kingdom at the time and arguing that the reduction of morality to the subjective was crippling society's ability to exercise moral courage in the midst of evil.

Lewis's words were chillingly prophetic about the present day. For example, take the polls that indicate people in the culture are increasingly uncomfortable with abortion on demand, yet the same polls indicate they are more likely to drive a friend to an abortion clinic to assist them in having an abortion. Or take the growing awareness of and opposition to human trafficking and sexual slavery, particularly on the part of people under the age of thirty-five. Yet they also are taught that pornography is supported by the right to free expression and ought to be viewed as morally neutral. They often don't see that such widespread acceptance of pornography is what fuels the demand around the world for prostitution and helps create the market for sex trafficking.

THE CASE FOR OBJECTIVE MORALITY

The idea that morality is objective and corresponds with the way things ought to be in a moral universe is often called "moral realism" by philosophers. To put it a bit more technically, this is the view that moral facts exist and are independent of our attitudes and beliefs about them.[2] I use *moral realism* and *moral objectivism* (the view that moral values are objective, not subjective) interchangeably, though there are some technical differences between the two. For the most part, however, they are talking about the same thing — that there is such a thing as moral truth, or moral knowledge, and that it exists independently of how we feel about it.

Objective morality best corresponds to our commonsense way of talking about morality.[3] We typically don't talk about moral matters as though they are entirely subjective or relativistic. We use argument, debate, and good reasons for our moral views, assuming that moral discussion can be like other forms of debate and argument (unlike talking about someone's preference for flavors of ice cream). We commonly apply the laws of logic to moral discussion, and we regularly assess moral arguments as either valid or invalid. Philosopher Russ Shafer-Landau insists, "Were we convinced that there was no truth of the matter, most would see their continued disagreement as pointless; as pointless as, say, entering an intractable debate about whether red or orange was *really* the most beautiful color."[4] For those who don't believe there is a moral law that can be known, moral persuasion doesn't make any sense. Virtually everyone who engages in moral debate about substantial issues tends to act as though there is a right answer, either awaiting consensus or begging for persuasion. Clearly this would not be true for many more trivial issues, about which we can agree to disagree without serious consequences. But our commonsense way of talking about issues such as slavery, civil rights, human trafficking, and other injustices assumes a truth value to one's position. Objective morality makes the best sense of our passion to persuade others about the truth of our views on issues critical to our continuing life together in community. If morality is nothing more than an expression of our personal tastes and preferences, it is very difficult to make sense of the way we debate moral issues.

In addition, objective morality makes the best sense of how we commonly talk about moral mistakes.[5] Take, for example, someone like Hitler or Stalin or any of the other twentieth-century tyrants. When we charge someone like this with the kinds of monumental immorality that we sometimes do, we aren't simply saying their views are incoherent or their actions are based on moral views that are merely different. We are saying when we acknowledge their views are in error that they have made grave moral mistakes — that is, they have deviated from a moral truth that really exists. Unless there is such a thing as moral truth that can be known, it is difficult, if not impossible, to stand in judgment on the tyrants of history, which we have obviously done already. The converse of this is also true — that moral realism makes the best sense of how we talk about moral progress. Unless morality is objective, the notion of moral progress makes little sense. For the relativist, there is no such thing as moral progress, since the cultural consensus determines morality. Further, the very idea of moral progress assumes there is a standard by which progress, or lack of it, is measured.

Finally, objective morality best accounts for the "oughts" of ethics. If morality is a matter of subjective tastes and preferences, then it is very difficult to explain where the "ought to" of ethics comes from. Expressions of preference cannot give us moral norms, nor can desires give us moral values. Neither can the cultural consensus of the relativist give us those norms, since one cannot derive a moral norm simply from a description of the cultural consensus or one's moral preferences. To put it another way, moral psychology cannot give us normative ethical principles and virtues.

So if we accept that morality is objective and not fundamentally a human creation, that it is something discovered, not invented by human beings, that raises the question, "Where did it come from?" That is, how do we account for the origin of morality? Objective morality insists that moral values and virtues are hardwired into the world — they are a part of the world as it is, similar to the laws of physics and mathematics.

An increasingly common way of answering the question "Where did morality come from?" is provided by evolutionary biology. That is, instead of morality being "written on our hearts," morality is written on our genes, the product of evolutionary forces. Our moral instincts arose as a result of evolution, similar to the belief in our physical evolution. Sociobiologist E. O. Wilson insists that "ethical codes have arisen by evolution through the interplay of biology and culture."[6] He cites the parallels in behavior between animals and human beings and claims they originated similarly. "Each kind of animal is guided through its life cycle by unique and often elaborate sets of instinctual algorithms. We may reasonably conclude that human behavior originated the same way."[7] Wilson suggests that the coming debate over ethics will pit the "transcendentalists," as he calls them (or those who favor objective morality that has a transcendent source), against the empiricists (who see morality as having a purely material origin, namely in biological evolution). He says, "Ought is the product of a material process."[8] Philosopher Michael Ruse expresses the idea this way:

> The position of the modern evolutionist ... is that humans have an awareness of morality ... because such an awareness is of biological worth. Morality is a biological adaptation no less than are hands and feet and teeth.... Considered as a rationally justifiable set of claims about an objective something, ethics is illusory. I appreciate that when somebody says, "Love thy neighbor as thyself," they think they are referring above and beyond themselves.... Nevertheless, ... such reference is truly without foundation. Morality is just an aid to survival and reproduction ... and any deeper meaning is illusory.[9]

This is a somewhat different view than the relativism and subjectivism I have described throughout this chapter. In this view, morality could still be objective but not originating from a transcendent source such as God's commands or natural law. Moral behavior has thus evolved in human beings, because it is more advantageous to our survival living in large groups to have morality. Traits such as cooperation, respect, and civility are conducive to our survival and thus are passed on to succeeding generations in the form of moral norms and standards. These standards can evolve over time as the needs of societies change. So what might have been conducive to survival in one era might not be the case in another, and thus the standards are not necessarily unchangeable.

In the years to come, this evolutionary view of morality will likely increasingly challenge the view that morality has a transcendent source. And let's be clear so that we don't confuse this view with the idea of moral progress. In one sense, our moral discernment does change. For example, for the majority of the history of civilization, human beings have been enslaved, and for most of that time, there was little moral objection. But our changing consensus on slavery is an example of moral progress. Society's moral beliefs and practices improved as slavery was abolished around the world.[10]

In addition, views of women's rights, specifically women's gaining the right to vote, is an example of moral progress, whereby society's attitudes and actions both became more consistent with the mandate of equal rights for women. However, acknowledging our moral discoveries and progress is not the same thing as saying that morality itself — the moral standards — have necessarily evolved. Our application may look different at different times and in different cultures, but the standards (the principles and virtues) themselves are unchanging.

But what do we say to the notion that morality is "written on our genes"? Two responses may be helpful here. First, think about the moral virtues that don't seem to contribute to our ongoing survival at all and actually appear to undercut our survival. Think, for example, about self-sacrifice and heroism. We often link heroic behavior with extreme self-sacrifice that often results in the death of the hero. Think of the person who instinctively rushes into a burning building to save a child, not knowing if he or she will come out alive. Or take the driver who sees a car plunge into a river. He or she instinctively rushes into the water to save the people in the car without giving much thought to his or her own well-being. In the evolutionary view of morality, there is no place for the person who "lays down his life for another." He's wasted his life. Professor Glenn Sunshine pointedly says:

> Evolutionary psychology is based on the Darwinian principle of natural selection. Natural selection occurs within a species. It is me, out competing someone else that is human to pass my genes down to the next generation. That is the principle behind Darwinism. *Under those circumstances the Marine who throws himself on the grenade is a loser.* He does not pass his genes down to the next generation. His competitors in the platoon get to do that. He is a loser. Are you willing to say that? Does your moral sense tell you that his self-sacrifice is the act of someone who is not fit to survive? If the answer is no, then you've got an internal incoherence in your analysis.

Chuck Colson described a similar act of self-sacrifice offered on his behalf when he was in prison following the Watergate scandal.

> It is important to understand in a completely materialistic universe if we are simply programmed by our genes, if we are not in control of ourselves, then the highest ethical obtainment is survival. *But the world works just the other way.* When I was in prison, and I had a lot of personal problems, and my dad had died. A lot of things went wrong. My son was arrested. A man in my prayer group, who was then a senior United States Congressman, called the president of the United States, then Gerald Ford, and said, "I would like to go in and serve the rest of Chuck Colson's prison

sentence so he can go home." That is an extremely unselfish act. That wasn't programmed by his genes. That was by his love for me. I have seen it in my own daughter, who is a single mom raising an autistic child, devoting herself totally to this other person, and this is the whole thing of agape love.

What Colson and Sunshine are suggesting is that our everyday human experience of many moral values and virtues, such as self-sacrifice and unconditional love (two of the most universally recognized and highest virtues), do not seem consistent with the notion that morality is generated by evolutionary survival.

Nor does an evolutionary view of morality seem to square with the idea that human beings are free moral agents with real free choices — as opposed to our choices being somehow determined by our genetic makeup. In contrast to E. O. Wilson's earlier analogy with animals' moral instincts (their instinctual algorithms) being parallel to those of human beings, human beings make free choices and as a result are morally accountable in ways that animals are not. Michael Miller of the Acton Institute explains: "We experience ourselves as moral agents with freedom.... I'll give you an earthy example. A dog makes decisions, but they don't make free choices. A dog looks at the food in front of them, and says, 'There's a lion back there. I won't eat it, because I don't want to get eaten by the lion.' But no dog looks at another dog and thinks, 'Wow! She is beautiful, but I think I'll wait until marriage.' That doesn't happen."

Philosopher William Lane Craig says this about our freedom and moral accountability:

If there is no mind distinct from the brain (which is the case in a materialist view of a human being), then everything we think and do is determined by the input of our five senses and our genetic makeup. There is no personal agent who freely decides to do something. But without freedom, none of our choices is morally significant. They are like the jerks of a puppet's limbs, controlled by the strings of sensory

> input and physical constitution. And what moral value does
> a puppet or its movements have?[11]

That is, on an evolutionary view of morality and its corresponding materialist view of the world, concepts like genuine freedom to choose and the accompanying accountability are both illusions devoid of adequate grounding.

So if there are good reasons to think that morality is objective and can be known, and that moral claims are capable of being true or false, and if there are reasons to be skeptical that morality is written on our genes, then how do we account for the origin of morality? This is where a Christian worldview can provide a coherent account of where objective morality comes from. A view of morality is a part of every worldview, whether it is based on some kind of religion or some secular philosophy. In other words, since everyone has a worldview, everyone has a view of morality, though the degree to which it is thought out varies widely.

The view of objective morality that the Bible assumes is part of what I referred to in chapter 1 as the natural law tradition. What this means is that God embedded morality in his world as a part of his creation. That is, God structured morality into the world he made in the same way he ordained the laws of physics and mathematics. The Bible indicates that there is a fixed order of physical laws that govern the universe (Jer. 31:35 – 36; 33:20 – 21, 25 – 26), which is reflected in some of the psalms that disclose God's general revelation, such as Psalm 19: "The heavens declare the glory of God; the skies proclaim the work of his hands" (v. 1). The wisdom literature puts this in terms of God's embedding wisdom in his creation. For example, Proverbs maintains that God's wisdom was structured into his world, and human beings' exercise of dominion over the world includes unlocking what God has fixed into it (Proverbs 3:19 – 20; 8:22 – 31). Proverbs 8:32 – 36 makes clear that it is *moral* wisdom that is entrenched in God's world, for the admonition there is a moral one:

> Now then, my children, listen to me;
> blessed are those who keep my ways.

Listen to my instruction and be wise;
do not disregard it.
Blessed are those who listen to me,
watching daily at my doors,
waiting at my doorway.
For those who find me find life
and receive favor from the LORD.
But those who fail to find me harm themselves;
all who hate me love death.

This is very similar language to the moral advice throughout Deuteronomy, based on the specially revealed law of God. In Proverbs, however, it is based on the law of God embedded in his world. The Bible seems to have a play on words with this idea that God's wisdom is *engraved* in his world, since the term for "fixed order" (often translated "decree," Heb. *huqqāh*; Jer. 31:35 – 36) is the same term used in the Old Testament law for "statute" (Lev. 18:3 – 4). Scripture seems to be making a parallel between what God has literally engraved in his law (a reference to the tablets of the Mosaic law) and what he has figuratively engraved in his world. That is, what is engraved in the world is moral wisdom analogous to what is engraved on the tablets of the Law. Thus God engraved an objective moral order into his world and wrote it on the hearts of human beings (Rom. 2:14 – 16), thereby giving them an innate moral sense. Of course, God also gave human beings moral values and virtues in his Word, through what theologians commonly call "special revelation." Ethics is primarily the task of discerning, or discovering, right and wrong both from God's Word and God's world.

♪ The Founding Fathers of our nation essentially espoused this view of natural law and morality in the Declaration of Independence. From the very first line — "We hold these truths to be self-evident, that all men are created equal, that they are endowed by their Creator with certain unalienable rights, that among these are life, liberty, and the pursuit of happiness" — they conveyed that the fundamental rights they were protecting (equality, life, liberty, and the pursuit of happiness) were endowed by our Creator and were both self-evident and inalienable (they could not be forfeited or taken away). They held that these rights were built into the fabric of the world. They understood well that government did not endow human beings with these rights, since rights bestowed by the state could just as easily be confiscated by that same state. They also held that they were self-evident, by which they meant that they were so clear it is expected that everyone would recognize them without a need for any additional argument about the matter.

GOD AND MORALITY

Certainly from a Christian worldview, belief in God and objective morality are closely connected. An objective moral law is consistent with the idea that God embedded objective morality in his world and has given human beings the tools to uncover those values and virtues. Special revelation in the Bible clarifies those moral principles and character traits in addition to providing all we need when it comes to matters of salvation and eternity. In fact, if God exists, then the ideas of morality and moral accountability make sense in a way one cannot claim about nontheistic views of the world. If God doesn't exist, then morality is nothing more than a human convention or evolutionary survival instinct, making morality entirely subjective and nonbinding.

Moral language may be used to describe things that society thinks are good ideas, but they are nothing more than that. Anyone who acts differently is not doing anything wrong, just being a nonconformist. Yet, as we have seen, that's not the way we live or the way we talk about morality. This is part of what I mean when I say the culture has an incoherent view of morality. Philosopher Richard Taylor pointedly says:

> The modern age, more or less repudiating the idea of a divine lawgiver, has nevertheless tried to retain the ideas of moral right and wrong, not noticing that, in casting God aside, they have also abolished the conditions of meaningfulness for moral right and wrong as well.... Contemporary

writers in ethics, who blithely discourse upon moral right and wrong and moral obligation without any reference to religion, are really just weaving intellectual webs from thin air; which amounts to saying that they discourse without meaning.[12]

That is, these contemporary ethics philosophers are simply giving opinions devoid of moral value.

To be clear, I'm not asking, "Can someone live a moral life without belief in God?" or "Can someone have a system of ethics without belief in God?" Certainly both of those things are possible. There are numerous examples of fine moral people who do not believe in God or hold to a Christian worldview. It is surely the case that some atheists are more moral than some Christians. Moreover, it is entirely possible to have a system of ethics without belief in God. Systems such as utilitarianism (morality is determined by the consequences of one's actions — those who produce the greatest good for the greatest number of people are moral) or ethical egoism (morality is determined by that which advances one's self-interest) are examples of moral systems not at all dependent on theism. The question we are entertaining in this section is this: Can objective morality be adequately grounded apart from God existing?

If God does not exist, then there is no such thing as objective morality. Yet we have seen that objective morality makes the best sense out of how we live and talk about morality, especially when we are the victims of injustice and when we make moral judgments, which we do routinely. C. S. Lewis, in *Mere Christianity*, argued for a universal moral law and maintained that only with a being such as God did objective morality make sense.[13] If it is true that morality is objective and not a human creation, as I have already suggested, then either there is a moral lawgiver (something like God), or objective morality has always existed and could even be eternal. This is the view of some philosophers and even goes back to the ancient Greeks, such as Plato, who held that the Good just existed and did not necessarily require a god or gods who had ordained it.[14] Keep in mind, however, that Plato did not have a materialist view of the world at all. He believed there was much more to the world than merely its physical stuff. He actually held that the Good was something basic and intrinsic to the world — that it was part of the structure of the world. For some, this view that objective morality has always existed somehow seems more rational than believing God is the moral lawgiver behind the moral law. But that is no less a step of faith than it is to believe God ordained morality. It is far more plausible to believe a moral God invested his world with moral properties and obligations than it is to believe moral obligations are just part of the world we live in.

Think about it this way. If there is no God and all that exists is the material universe (this is the worldview of philosophical naturalism, sometimes referred to as materialism), and it is the result of chance, directionless forces of evolution, then there is no adequate way to account for moral properties such as obligations, right and wrong, and the guilt universally felt when failing those obligations. C. S. Lewis said it like this: "[What] I have got to believe in is a Something which is directing the universe, and which appears in me as a law urging me to do right and making me feel responsible and uncomfortable when I do wrong. I think we have to assume it is more like a mind than it is like anything else we know, because after all the only other thing we know is matter, and *you can hardly imagine a bit of matter giving instructions.*"[15] If not on an evolutionary basis, it is not obvious where the nature of moral obligation comes from in a purely material universe. Without a moral lawgiver, notions of right and wrong are merely human conventions and have no universally binding qualities about them. Objective and binding moral properties that fit the way we live and talk about morality simply do not follow from a materialist view of the world. This is what Yale law professor Arthur Leff describes as the "grand sez who" when it comes to moral demands. In a materialist worldview, there is no adequate answer to that question. Leff correctly describes the "death of God" movement as also the death of normative ethics and legal systems, a movement from "an exultant 'We're free of God' to a despairing 'Oh God, we're free.'"[16]

Here's another way to think about this. In a materialistic world, where the material stuff of the world is all there is, there is nothing else beside this life. In addition, we live in a world where we experience moral obligations and judgments when we fail to live up to those obligations. Further, we experience many moral obligations, which in the materialist world result in net losses of benefit to those who keep them (for example, the moral obligation to rescue someone in need, to repay a debt, to keep a promise, or to refrain from stealing; in fact, you could make a good case that most of our moral obligations conflict with our self-interest, which is why we often refer to moral tension as "temptation"). Nevertheless, if the person fails to keep an obligation, he or she is subject to judgment, if not shame, and the greater the failure, the greater the sense that the person is somehow defective in character. But having those obligations only makes sense if, as philosopher George Mavrodes puts it, "reality itself is committed to morality in some deep way. It makes sense only if there is moral demand on the world too, and only if reality will in the end satisfy that demand."[17] And reality, on a materialist view of the world, cannot satisfy that demand. That is, the radical demands of morality that most often bring losses to one's life when viewed from the materialist view of the world seem absurd. Unless there is a moral lawgiver who has invested the world with morality and who provides a framework for the demands of morality resulting in good to the one who upholds them, the demands of morality make little sense. This is precisely what a Christian worldview does for the enterprise of morality — it makes sense of the moral world we both live in and talk about.

Conclusion

I have tried to make the case for objective morality and a moral lawgiver as that which makes the best sense of how we live in our moral universe and how we commonly talk about morality. I have suggested that God embedded objective morality into his world (natural law) and clarified it in his Word (special revelation), both of which support and reinforce the other. I suggested that if God doesn't exist, then the case for an adequately grounded objective morality is in serious jeopardy, and there is no adequate way to answer the "grand sez who" question about moral obligation. If there is no God who grounds our moral obligations, then we are left with the incoherence of morality described in chapter 1. Law professor Arthur Leff describes the incoherence:

> As things now stand (without God grounding morality), everything is up for grabs. Nevertheless:
> Napalming babies is bad.
> Starving the poor is wicked.
> Buying and selling each other is depraved.
> Those who stood up to and died resisting Hitler, Stalin, Amin, and Pol Pot—and General Custer too—have earned salvation.
> Those who acquiesced deserve to be damned.
> There is in the world such a thing as evil.
> (All together now:) Sez who?
> God help us.[18]

CHAPTER 3

If We Know What's Right, Can We Do It?

Is it possible to foster virtuous behavior, and if so, how is that done? After my concluding in chapter 1 that there is a crisis in ethics today, you might be cynical about the prospects for virtue. But if it is true that there is moral law that can be known, which I concluded in chapter 2, that makes the questions addressed in this chapter very challenging. If we can know what is right, do we have what it takes to do it consistently so that it becomes habitual?

Chuck Colson, one of the key figures in the Watergate scandal that brought down the Nixon administration in the 1970s, faced this question directly with some very dramatic consequences. Here's how he described his experience:

> When President Nixon asked me to leave my law firm in Washington and come in and be his Special Counsel, the first thing I did was to be certain there'd be no conflicts of interest. I took everything I had earned as a lawyer; I put it in a blind trust. I told my law partners not to come visit me,

and they didn't. I was certain that I would never be compromised. I was determined not to be, because Washington is a city filled with scandals. I had been raised this way.... I'd learned about duty and honor, and I learned about integrity as a Marine....

Being honest, this was a big thing with me. I would get gifts at Christmastime, for example, and I would take them down to the White House switchboard operators, or the guys that drove my cars, because I was never going to be compromised.

And I was so determined, I ended up going to prison. Why? I think you can be so self-righteous that you don't see what's really going on. You become oblivious to your own insensitivities, because you're sure nobody can compromise you. Human beings have the infinite capacity of self-rationalization, and that's exactly what I did....

I can think back on times that I remember. When there were four or five of us in the office, and the president was exploding over something that had gotten out. It was in the hands of the Brookings Institution, and he turned to Bob Haldeman. He said, "Bob, have we got a team in place that can go in and get those documents back (referring to the Watergate break-in)? Remember, I've asked you for that?" *Then I later realized, that was a time when I should have stopped and said, "Wait a minute Mr. President. Think about the consequences of this,"* but I did not. Self-righteousness is believing that you're so good that you couldn't be compromised. That's the kind of pride that's fatal, and was in my life, because I was so sure of myself, that I didn't realize how vulnerable I was, as every human being is.

Colson's experience with Watergate reminds us of how susceptible we all are to moral failure. Even though he had strong moral upbringing with the lessons his parents imprinted on him, he failed. He realized how our capacity for rationalization and self-deception is virtually infinite and that all of us are capable of a wide variety of ethical lapses. Our vulnerability to moral malfunction makes this chapter even more important. Since we can know what is right, and since we are so vulnerable to doing what is wrong, it is crucial that we understand how to cultivate virtue so it becomes habitual in our lives. Without making it too depressing an exercise, think back about the moral blunders you've made in your own life. How did those things happen? What went wrong? Maybe you wondered, *How did I get into this mess?* and concluded that it occurred a few small steps at a time, and over time you ended up in a much different place than you ever imagined, having rationalized that each small step was no big deal. Or maybe the pressures of the workplace or some other arena clouded your judgment, as was the case with Colson in the White House. Or it may be that your passions simply took over and overpowered your ability to think clearly about the situation, which is what happens to many people who succumb to sexual temptation.

WHY BE VIRTUOUS?

Ancient philosophers such as Plato and Aristotle had a lot to say about ethics, particularly what has come to be called "virtue ethics." They defended an idea we have only assumed so far, that being moral, or being virtuous, is actually a good and desirable thing that ought to be pursued. But not everybody agrees with that today. Some people hold that being virtuous is for chumps or losers, that in a dog-eat-dog world where you have to look out for number one, being moral holds you back. This is the worldview popularized by the reality TV show *Survivor.* And it is sometimes expressed by Donald Trump and the participants in his show, *The Apprentice.* So how would you answer the question "Why be moral?"

We have already seen that good ethics are critical for a properly functioning society, particularly one that holds freedom in such high regard. Most people would not want to live in a society in which morality was unimportant, in which conceptions of right and wrong carried little weight. In fact, it is unlikely that any civilized society could continue unless it had concern for important moral values such as fairness, justice, truthfulness, and compassion. Most people seem to recognize intuitively that there is something important for the culture about people being good. Ethics are essential because they give direction to people and societies who have some sense that they cannot flourish without being moral.

Free societies require virtuous people capable of the self-restraint morality provides. In fact, when the notion of freedom was articulated centuries ago, it was not freedom to do whatever you wanted to do, it was freedom *to do what you thought was right*, what your conscience dictated to you was right. Only more recently has the idea of freedom been divorced from virtue and degenerated into autonomy almost without limits. Michael Miller points out, "If we are going to have self-government, we need to be self-governors." And that means we must cultivate the virtues that enable people to practice the habits necessary for free societies to flourish.

That helps answer the big-picture question "Why should society (everyone else) be moral?" But let's be more specific and ask, "Why should *I* be moral?" How would you respond to that question? Most people, when they are genuinely honest with themselves, associate doing well in life with being a good person. Having moral character is still essential to most people's conceptions of what makes a person flourish in his or her life. For example, it is difficult to imagine a person being considered a success in life if she has gained her wealth dishonestly. It is equally difficult to call a person a success who is at the top of his profession but cheats on his wife, abuses his children, and drinks too much. On the other hand, we rightly hold up someone like Mother Teresa as a model of a person having lived a good life, even though she lacked most material goods society values. One of the principal reasons for being moral is that being a good person is central to most concepts of human fulfillment. For the Christian, being moral is critical to a life that seeks to honor God. Being moral is important because God highly recommends it! The reason he does, and the reason we can say that being moral is inherently good, is because it is foundational to a person's flourishing in life. Having a good life and being a good person still go hand in hand for most people.

The ancient philosophers were very clear in the way they understood this connection between virtue and a good life. In fact, this was the reason they saw ethics as such an important component of a person's overall approach to life. Socrates, when describing the importance of ethics, said, "We are discussing no small matter, but how we ought to live." Similarly, Plato held that being a good person was inherently valuable apart from any benefits it produced for a person. In his classic story "The Myth of Gyges," Gyges was given the chance to live as an invisible person; he could do anything he wanted with the assurance he would never be caught or held accountable for any of it. Plato pressed the question that if a person could get away with everything he ever wanted to do, would a person want to be moral, and if so, why? He concluded that being virtuous was intrinsically valuable and critical to a good life. For Plato, the notion of justice, or integrity, was not necessarily something a person did but was a condition of a person's soul. In his best-known work, *The Republic*, he compared the soul to the city, calling the city "a soul writ large." He maintained that a just city is a city that is functioning properly, with all people fulfilling the roles they are designed to fulfill, all doing their parts with excellence. He argued that integrity is parallel to this — with the component parts of a person's soul all functioning according to their designed function, with reason controlling the passions. The person who has his or her soul in order in this way is said to have justice in the soul. Thus justice is not primarily something you *do*, but is something you *are*. It is a condition of one's soul first and an action one performs second. This is why Plato connected integrity and a good life. He held that if your soul is in disarray, you not only lack integrity, but you can't possibly have a good life. Of course, a just person was also expected to perform just actions, but what is important here is to recognize that the idea of justice for Plato is an overall condition of a person's inner life. This is parallel to what Dallas Willard calls "the well-ordered heart."[1] And this is what we sometimes mean when we say a person "has it together," referring to his or her inner life that is in order.

Other ancient philosophers echoed this understanding of ethics being about a person's whole life. This is why they made the connection between virtue and happiness so easily. For example, Aristotle maintained that virtue was essential to happiness. He went a bit further than Plato — he was more specific in what the virtues were and how they were derived. He made this connection between happiness and virtue: "Happiness is an activity of soul in accordance with virtue." The Roman philosopher Epicurus, who came along after Aristotle, said it clearly too: "It is not possible to live pleasantly without living prudently, honorably, and justly." You might be familiar with Epicurus — he's the one for whom the philosophy of Epicureanism is named. But what you might not know is that the "eat, drink, and be merry" hedonistic view of life commonly associated with Epicureanism actually has nothing to do with his philosophy. I suspect he turns over in his grave when he hears this association of hedonism with his views! He believed that to flourish in a difficult world required virtue and prudence. He saw virtue as a critical element to living well. These philosophers certainly echo what Jesus taught when he said, "What good is it for someone to gain the whole world, yet forfeit their soul?" (Mark 8:36).

Despite the understandable cynicism about virtue in the culture today, I think we still believe virtue and a good life are connected, that there is something important about being a good person. For example, my longtime teaching colleague in the business school at Biola University tells about the time when this link between virtue and a good life first made sense to him. He was an attorney in his late twenties, just a few years out of law school, in a large firm in a major metropolitan area. One of the partners in the firm was one of the best-known trial lawyers in the country in his specific legal field (tort law). He was legendary for his courtroom successes, and when he took my colleague under his wing and wanted to mentor him as his successor, my friend was initially very flattered and thrilled with the opportunity. But as time went on, he got to know his mentor pretty well and got to see his life up close. He soon realized that this man had no friends, likely because he had alienated most of them over the years; was a hopeless workaholic, because that's all he had in his life; and had no family life. He had three broken marriages, and he was estranged from all of his children. As an example of how empty his life was, when he was discharged from the hospital after suffering a heart attack, the only person who was available, or wanted to be available, to take him home was his secretary! In fact, my colleague was one of the first people he called to see if he would bring him home. None of his wives or children were the least bit inclined to help in his time of critical need. Though he was certainly successful in terms of his wealth and position, it is not hard to conclude that he was a failure at life. As my graduate school mentor, Howard Hendricks, would say, "He climbed the ladder of success only to discover that it was leaning against the wrong wall!" My colleague drew the right conclusion when he realized that his mentor's life was not something to emulate. He left that firm when it became clear that the life he would lead would undermine his family life and ultimately his flourishing. He understood that a good life was more valuable than what he would accomplish and the money he would make. It included having good character (that is, having his soul in order) as a nonnegotiable element.

Similarly, out-of-control ambition nearly ruined the life of Dominic Orr, whose story was the focus of a provocative *Fortune* magazine cover story titled "Confessions of a CEO." Self-described as "ruthlessly aggressive," Orr was a classic workaholic. He was a successful CEO, taking two Silicon Valley tech companies public, but his career success cost him his marriage and nearly permanently alienated his two children. What finally awakened him to the fact that his life was careening out of control was the discovery that his son had taken a fireplace poker and his skateboard to his luxury car in a last-ditch attempt to get his attention. A painful nine-year journey that involved depression, therapy, and extended time out of the workplace eventually helped Orr regain perspective of what is meant by a good life. He returned to be CEO of another start-up company, chastened by his past hard-driving ways. He eventually realized that even though he was at the top of the corporate world, he was at the bottom of his personal life. He did make painful changes to his work life and regained his relationship with his two children, though, tragically, his marriage was beyond repair.[2]

By contrast, consider Mother Teresa, arguably one of the most universally admired figures in the world, whose legacy lives on since her death in 1997. For most of her life, she labored in obscurity, serving the poorest of the poor in the slums of Calcutta. Toward the end of her life, she began to receive recognition for her decades of selfless service, and she even won the Nobel Prize. (She gave all the money away!) She achieved nothing of what our culture considers necessary for a good life — not wealth, position, or fame (though she did become famous toward the end of her life, and somewhat against her will). From today's cultural view of success, we would conclude that she wasted her life. But for the ancient philosophers, and from a Christian worldview, her life was anything but a waste. It was precisely because of her character that we consider her life well lived.

BACK TO VIRTUE

The thinking of the ancient philosophers whom I have cited — Socrates, Plato, Aristotle, Epicurus, and others — was adopted and expanded by some of the best Christian philosophers of the early and medieval history of Christianity. Thinkers such as Augustine and Aquinas continued the tradition of virtue begun by the ancients and integrated it with the teachings of Christianity. For example, Aristotle placed great importance on having a moral example — someone who could model the virtues and be emulated. In Christian teaching, Jesus filled that role perfectly, being the ideal example of character. As a result, the New Testament emphasizes becoming like Jesus as the goal of a person's spiritual life. The fruit of the Spirit in Galatians 5:22 – 23 are the character traits of Jesus produced by the activity of the Holy Spirit in the life of the believer. For Augustine and Aquinas, the fruit of the Spirit continued the ancient tradition of connecting virtue and the good life but put it in distinctly Christian terms.

However, after medieval Christianity and with the coming of the Renaissance and the Enlightenment, there was a shift away from this emphasis on virtue toward a different formulation of ethics. Part of the reason for this change came from the more general movement in the Enlightenment away from religion, particularly Christianity, as the dominant way of viewing the world. Several different efforts were made to base morality on something beside Christian theology. One clear example is the utilitarian ethic of Jeremy Bentham and John Stuart Mill, which sought explicitly to determine right and wrong without appeal to God or the Bible but instead by appeal to the consequences of a particular action or moral rule. Similarly, Immanuel Kant sought to derive moral principles based on what he called the "categorical imperative," or the principle of universalizability, without explicit appeal to religious views (though Kant did believe that God was necessary ultimately to ground morality). By contrast, Thomas Hobbes sought to derive moral duties from our self-interested nature, leading to what is known today as ethical egoism. And David Hume grounded morality in what is immediately pleasing or agreeable, paving the way for moral subjectivism.

The overall difference in the way ethics was done in the Enlightenment was a move toward assessment of *actions* rather than character. Morality was viewed more as a way to help people make decisions about moral dilemmas than it was a guide to what constituted a good life. As a result, ethics became less tied to virtue and character and more about moral decision making. Unfortunately, one of the casualties of the Enlightenment collapse of the medieval Christian worldview was the virtue tradition of the ancients developed by Aquinas. It was the beginning of the secularization of ethics and has resulted in the relativism and subjectivism I have already discussed.

Recent years have seen an encouraging resurgence of interest in virtue ethics. Its proponents recognize that an ethic that only addresses decisions and dilemmas is incomplete. They aren't saying we don't ever need guidance to make moral decisions and resolve moral dilemmas, but today's virtue ethics insists there is much more to the moral life than that. They argue correctly that there is more to being moral than simply making the right decisions. They criticize what they call "action-oriented ethics" for emphasizing doing over being, following abstract moral rules instead of exemplary people, stressing actions over attitudes/ motives, and obeying rules over developing character. Ethics is reduced to solving hard cases and is moved to the extremes of life, rather than being part of the everyday life of the average person. They further point out that action-oriented ethics provide little motivation for doing the right thing, and that without motivation, moral obligations can become rigid and legalistic and essentially amount to a façade of morality to hide character defects. In addition, in keeping with the individualistic temper of the Enlightenment, action-oriented ethics overemphasize the ability of each person to arrive at his or her moral duties by reason and in isolation. The virtue tradition, by contrast, stresses the development of virtue in community. This continues Aristotle's emphasis that the virtues cannot be lived apart from the community, since the purpose for developing the virtues is to enable a person to live well in the community.

Philosopher Peter Kreeft argues that ethics without virtue is "ethics light." He suggests that what is taught in the university today is a truncated view of ethics that is divorced from character and can actually be dangerous. He says, "Ethics without virtue is a 'little morality.' ... Ethics without virtue is an illusion."[3] Similarly, Harvard professor Robert Coles, in his article "The Disparity between Intellect and Character," tells of a Harvard student who, in working her way through school by cleaning other students' rooms, recounted how students at the top of the class regularly treated her with contempt and how one in particular routinely hit on her sexually. The particular student had actually taken two of Coles's classes on moral reasoning and made As in both of them.

She asked the perceptive question about what is actually being taught and learned in ethics classes in the university. "What's the point of knowing good if you don't keep trying to become a good person?" she asked.[4]

Cultivating Virtue

So how do you become a good person? How do you connect the moral law we can know with actually doing it as a matter of habit? Our culture suggests various ways.[5] The first is by *rules and compliance.* This is the usual knee-jerk response to ethical scandals in business and has certainly been the response to the financial crisis of the past few years. Virtue is encouraged in the corporate world by multiplying rules and regulations, and by assuming that adhering to them is the same thing as developing virtue. For example, in my corporate ethics consulting work, I have had considerable resistance to the idea that compliance and ethics are not the same thing. At one point, I had a conversation with the "integrity" officer for a hospital for which I was doing consulting. She was operating under the assumption that what she was involved with was clearly ethics. So I asked her, "What exactly is your job as the integrity officer for the hospital?" She replied without hesitation, "My full-time job is to make sure that our top executives and managers don't go to jail." I replied, "I thought the bar for ethics was a bit higher than ending the calendar year without indictments being handed down!"

Of course the problem with adding a lot of rules is that they don't make us more inclined to follow the rules. Rather, they often make us more inclined to break them. They can actually make us better at finding loopholes so that we can technically follow the rules and still do what we want. Jesus repeatedly pointed out to the religious leaders of his day that multiplying the rules actually undermined virtue and one's relationship to God. He quoted from the prophet Isaiah, "These people honor me with their lips, but their hearts are far from me. They worship me in vain; their teachings are merely human rules" (Mark 7:6 – 7).

Often rules are put in place to protect us — that is, protect us from *others* who might want to do us harm. But the rules do not and cannot protect us from *ourselves*, in large part because one can follow the rules for all the wrong reasons and with all the wrong attitudes. This is why rules are so counter to the tradition of virtue and why philosophers through the ages have emphasized that morality is incomplete without the cultivation of virtue.

The culture's second strategy with regard to virtue is *incentives*. That is, incentives work to show us that being virtuous is in our self-interest. To put it more plainly, incentives attempt to buy us into cultivating virtue. For example, much of the discussion in business ethics revolves around the question of whether good ethics is also good business (in terms of profitability). Many people believe it is, and they use this to encourage ethical behavior in the marketplace. If you do the right thing, your actions will build trust and make you more profitable. In some instances, this is true. In the long run, it may be true more often than not. But think about this: if virtuous behavior were always good business, then the field of business ethics would be out of business! That's because everyone would do the right thing all the time unless they were stupid or shortsighted. The reason we have business ethics is because being virtuous often involves a cost. We often refer to ethical issues as "temptations," because that's precisely what they are. They involve a conflict between our self-interest and the demands of virtue, and the requirements of virtue generally ought to trump our self-interest.

Incentives don't often encourage virtue in a long-lasting way. The incentives in our culture do not encourage things like delaying gratification but rather press us to live for the here and now. They do not encourage sexual purity and marital faithfulness or generosity or moderation. And there is no reason to equate what's right with what's in our self-interest. If that could be done, then cultivating virtue would be exponentially easier than it is and would not require the discipline to develop those habits.

A third strategy of the culture to produce good people is *education*. We commonly assume that if people are not doing what is right, it must be because they are uninformed and in need of education. Underlying this assumption is the notion that if people know the right thing to do, they will do it. But just as there is no inherent connection between success and being a good person, there is no link between being educated and being a good person. D. L. Moody once said, "If you take someone who steals railroad ties and give him an education, all you've done is teach him to steal the entire railroad." This is because education is often technical and does not deal with training in character. Increasingly, college graduates are entering the workplace with good educations, degrees in hand, good jobs, and their whole life in front of them, and they are miserable. This phenomenon has been called the "quarter-life crisis" because it begins in one's mid- to late twenties. It has spawned books, a blog, and a website that encourage men and women in their twenties and early thirties to record their experience, get support, and gain insight.[6] These young people have been well educated, but that education did not include insight into why they are pursuing their careers and how they can become good people. A Duke University student quoted in Steven Garber's book *The Fabric of Faithfulness* summarized it like this: "We've got no philosophy of what it is we want by the time somebody graduates. The so-called curriculum is a set of hoops that somebody says students ought to jump through before graduation. *Nobody seems to have asked, 'How do people become good people?'*"[7] This is why education in most secular universities cannot be the way virtue is cultivated, because it simply doesn't include matters of character and how that contributes to a good life. As my graduate school mentor put it, "All education does for us is to make us smarter sinners."[8]

A fourth way our culture attempts to foster virtue is by urging us to *look inside ourselves*. Though it is true that the unexamined life is not worth living, attempting to find your moral compass by looking inside yourself is an ironic way to do that. I have said already that the conscience is not infallible and needs to be trained, and that the conscience is broken just like all other parts of a person's nature. But imagine that you tried to use a compass to find your way out of being lost — but you had a magnet on your back, which meant the compass was always pointed at you! It would be useless to help you find your way. What makes a field compass effective is the same thing that makes a moral compass effective — it points to a fixed reference point outside yourself (God's moral law, which can be known) and tells you where you are.

Cultivating virtue is not a simple task but the project of a lifetime. It begins by recognizing that being good and living a good life are integrally connected. It proceeds by small steps and decisions that develop the *habits* of virtue. The ancient philosophers understood that this involves practice and discipline so that the virtues become habitual. Aristotle, for example, spoke of reason governing the passions as critical to having a good life. More recently C. S. Lewis described the cultivation of virtue as the development of "the chest" of a person. "It still remains true that no justification of virtue will enable a man to be virtuous. Without the aid of trained emotions, the intellect is powerless against the animal organism.... As the King governs by his executive, so reason in man must rule the mere appetites by means of the 'spirited element.' *The head rules the belly through the chest* — the seat of the emotions organized by trained habit into stable sentiments."[9]

Lewis, back in the 1940s, lamented that what culture and education are producing today are "men without chests." That is, to be without a chest is to be without the ability to train one's emotions so that the passions can be controlled and thereby do not rule one's life. Lewis prophetically argued that education has left the culture devoid of the ability to cultivate virtue, precisely what we have seen through the experience of college students mentioned earlier in this chapter. Lewis maintained that the result is this tension between the need to have good people in society and the loss of the ability to produce them. He said, "In a sort of ghastly simplicity we remove the organ and demand the function. *We make men without chests and expect of them virtue and enterprise. We laugh* at honor and are shocked to find traitors in our midst. We castrate and bid the geldings be fruitful."[10]

Let's be more specific about how virtue is cultivated. First, it begins with families. The primary training ground for character is at home as parents teach and model virtue for their children. This is part of the sacred task of parenting and why even with the fracturing of the family today, parents remain the best hope for cultivating virtue in the next generation. Other institutions can come alongside families and assist in this, such as schools, churches, and other voluntary organizations like the Boy Scouts or Girl Scouts, the YMCA, youth sports, and many others. But the ultimate responsibility for cultivating virtue in children rests with families. Churches, for example, should not become a substitute for parents teaching and modeling virtue. Churches should actually be equipping families to instill character in their children.

What begins in families must be reinforced with accountability. The virtues are lived in community, not in isolation. Though it is true that a person's character is who he or she is when no one is looking, virtue does not happen in seclusion. Chuck Colson described the importance of accountability in his life:

> Let me give you one practical suggestion. I did not find this out until I hit my head and went to prison, and my meteoric career went down the drain. *I have to hold myself accountable to other people.* My wife, my immediate family, and my kids. I wouldn't think of making a decision without them. And I have got a smaller accountability group; half a dozen people. And I won't make any move without their concurrence. *I don't trust myself.* That is a good place for me to start. Find five or six friends and form an accountability group.

This accountability is critical among the men and women in prison — thousands of whom Colson has counseled over the years. The Prison Fellowship ministry Colson founded, which has an element of strict accountability, has produced some significant results when it comes to recidivism. He reported, "The national statistics are that 60 percent re-offend within three years. Our [Prison Fellowship] graduates, and this has been consistent across the board, 8 percent. So you can really build character." And when asked what makes the difference, Colson was clear about the answer: "It's accountability to one another."

A third critical element in cultivating virtue is the practice of repentance. Since we all are capable of self-deception (some might say we are actually quite skilled at it!) and moral failure, repentance is a necessary part of character formation. This assumes humility and a basic distrust of ourselves and our motives. But repentance does more than remind us of our past failures; it helps us exercise our habits of virtue by pointing us in the direction of virtue. I have found there are few more powerful ways to model virtue in my family than to admit to my wife and children when I have made a mistake. For me to come clean with them when I blow it not only tells them I am human, but it points them toward the right by showing them exactly where I failed and what I want to do differently in the future. It is my relationship with them that also reinforces my desire to live virtuously among them, not wanting to hurt those whom I love the most.

Many of the prisoners Colson and others have worked with over many years have powerful stories of moral conversion — deciding to change the way they were living their lives and to commit themselves to developing character. What these stories show is that character can be developed, and it is done in community, with accountability. Listen to how these inmates involved in Prison Fellowship talk about what they've done to merit prison time and the changes they are making. Hear the resolve in their voices as they recount the decisions they've made to become better people.

My name is Sterling Knox. I'm serving 120 months for second-degree unintentional murder. I was too lazy and impatient to earn money like a real man. So I chose to rob people of more than their material possessions, but also their peace of mind. I destroyed a community [that I grew up in] and betrayed my family with my part in the senseless murder of [redacted].... What the [Prison Fellowship] community means to me is that I can be me and I can open myself up for others to see who I want to be and who I want to leave behind and give them the opportunity to help usher me to my goals.... I'm going to live my life with integrity and do the difficult right thing.

My name is Steve Janesek. I'm serving one hundred months for a cruel, cowardly, senseless act of assault. Forever have I victimized the people involved in [my crimes], giving them a life sentence of fear and instability, trust issues, that they probably will never overcome.... From here on out I'm going to be the person that people say this is what you can be rather than this is what you do not want to be.

My name is Bill. I am serving eighty-eight months for secondary possession of methamphetamines. I affected my community, my family, society as a whole.... Living in a community of other brothers who are changing, I have a sense of freedom where I can open up my heart to others. I think of the other people who are coming in [to prison]. One of the greatest gifts we can give each other is inspiration [to become better people].... From here on out, I want to be the man and the father that my children need. I want to be somebody that my old friends and my current friends can say "this is the man we respect." [I] can see some difference already in relation to [my] son. When my son got arrested, and I had to figure out number one, do I have any credibility with my son to be able to talk to him? I called him on his way up here and asked him if he knew why he was coming up here. And he said, because I am in trouble. I said, do you understand that I am not mad at you? That I just want to help you? He was able to identify through the questions I asked him the poor choices that he was making and friends he had chosen. And since that day there have been legal problems. But he's not hanging around with those friends. He's back on track with schoolwork. He's listening to his mother. I have my son back. I think for the first time he actually knew that his dad cared about him. He knows that I love him.

Virtue in a Christian Worldview

Many of the prisoners who experienced profound moral change also had a spiritual conversion. They would say that coming to faith in Christ was a critical part of their character formation. Bill said, "I have a renewed faith in Christ, and it helps me to refocus on what's important. And I've spent enough time taking away from other people. God's given me a lot of gifts, and it's time for me to put them to better use instead of manipulating other people for self-seeking issues." And Steve, when asked what makes him want to care about right and wrong today, said, "Knowing that there's a God there and he's forgiven me and that shows me love every day and knowing what it is to love one another and have compassion and empathy for another human being, and no longer following a corrupt belief system that is nothing but causing harm and pain to other people." Putting the cultivation of virtue within a distinctively Christian worldview makes the journey clearer, but it also raises some profound questions about the connection between Christian faith and virtue.

Christian faith clarifies our understanding of the life of virtue in at least three important ways. The first is that Christianity spells out specifically what the virtues are and provides a model for what a life of virtue looks like. The virtues are the character traits of Jesus, made evident in his earthly life and explained by the apostle Paul as the fruit of the Spirit (Gal. 5:22 – 23). Jesus furnished his followers with a model of the ideal person of virtue. One of the difficulties that plagues many non-Christian accounts of virtue is how to determine what the virtues are and what they are based on. Aristotle tried to explain the virtues with his Golden Mean — the virtue was the mean between two extremes. For example, courage is the mean between the two extremes of cowardice and rashness. Other virtue theorists have attempted to ground the virtues in some account of human nature. Sometimes it seems that proponents of virtue can't define the virtues but insist that they know a virtuous person when they see one. A Christian worldview provides a well-defined account of what makes a virtue a virtue and links it to the example provided by Jesus. Ultimately, developing a life of virtue consists of faithfully becoming more like Jesus, developing the habits of emulating him.

A second element a Christian worldview gives to our understanding of virtue is a more profound motive for cultivating character. As I mentioned earlier, the Christian answer to the question "Why be moral?" is that God highly recommends it. Ultimately, the motive for a life of virtue is that it is pleasing to God and is the only appropriate response to his overwhelming grace in our lives; it's not to earn God's favor but is because of his unconditional favor toward us. The decision to follow Jesus is fundamentally a decision to become like him, living that out in the community of God's people and in the surrounding culture.

A Christian worldview also connects the life of virtue to a vision of the good life, which in a Christian worldview involves knowing Jesus, becoming more like him, and living to serve in his kingdom. This definition of the good life as knowing Jesus provides an important relational component to the motive for virtue. Ultimately the reason I want to develop the habits of virtue and avoid the patterns of vice is not because of guilt or shame or some abstract notion of morality. *It is because I don't want to hurt someone I love — my Savior, Jesus.* I often ask my married students a question that brings this home to them: "What is it that keeps you faithful to your spouse?" I suggest that it is not primarily because adultery is wrong — though it clearly is. Nor is it because their spouses have threatened them with bodily harm if they cheat — that may or may not be true! Nor is it that they will likely be overwhelmed with guilt. The most compelling reason is that they don't want to hurt those they love — their spouses and children. This is what the Bible calls "godly sorrow" for sin, in contrast to guilt and self-condemnation, which is the common response to moral failure. The Bible indicates that there is no longer any condemnation for the believer, and thus the self-condemnation that so often accompanies moral failure has no place in the believer's spiritual experience (Rom. 8:1).

A third element a Christian worldview provides for virtue is the most important. Christian faith takes our fallen nature very seriously, and it is not assumed that if you know the right thing to do that you will do it. In fact, the Bible asserts the converse of that — that often knowing the right thing to do makes it less likely, not more, that you will actually do it. This seems to be the heart of Paul's teaching in Romans 7: there is an *inverse relationship* between knowing the right thing and doing it. As a result, the Bible insists that becoming like Jesus involves a combination of our choices and decisions and the transforming activity of God's Spirit (Rom. 8:12 – 13; 2 Cor. 3:17 – 18; Gal. 5:16 – 18). The life of virtue is referred to as the fruit of *the Spirit* because it is the activity of God's Spirit in conjunction with our habits, choices, and disciplines.

This intersection of virtue and a Christian worldview also raises some profound and puzzling questions. The most basic of these is simply, "Can a person be good without God?" This question needs to be clarified before attempting an answer. If what is meant by this is a more philosophical question — Can a person have an adequate grounding for moral values and virtues without God? — I have already said in chapter 2 that the answer is a resounding no. But if the meaning is whether a person can be good without a saving relationship with God, that's a different question, and the answer is yes. A person who does not know Christ can certainly exhibit virtuous traits and behaviors and can even be considered a good person. Devout people of other faiths are good examples of this — someone like Gandhi, for example.

I suspect you know people who are not Christians but who live good lives, maybe even better lives than many Christians you know. Someone might object that the Bible says there is no one who is good and no one who seeks after God (Rom. 3:10 – 12). But this is not intended in an absolute sense, that no one apart from Christ ever does anything good. Rather, no one is good in the sense that his or her goodness is sufficient to merit salvation from God. In other words, a person can be good, but not good enough to earn salvation. Thus it is possible for a person to be virtuous without saving grace, but that virtue is not enough to warrant being justified before God. Justification comes only by receiving the free gift of salvation from a perfect and gracious Savior, Jesus. This is why in addition to encouraging people to cultivate virtue, we also need to share with them the good news of the gospel of Jesus.

A second question then comes to mind: Do we have sufficient motive for virtue apart from a relationship with God? Similar to the previous question, it seems possible that a person could be motivated to cultivate character apart from, or prior to, conversion to Christianity. As we have seen with the changes made by the prisoners in the Prison Fellowship program, these changes of heart seem genuine, and the desire to live differently once out of prison is real. But it is also clear that a religious conversion provides resources and a level of motivation that give substantial help along the way in cultivating virtue. It is possible to have a conception of the good life that can motivate a life of virtue. After all, the ancient philosophers had a fairly well developed conception of the good life and how integral virtue was to achieving it. And it is a good thing to encourage people in the culture to live virtuous lives. But they also need the good news of the gospel of Christ in order to have a fully grounded view of the good life and the corresponding place of virtue in it.

A third question may sound a bit like the first two: Can a person have genuine moral reform without a religious conversion? Again, the testimony of the Prison Fellowship program inmates seems to indicate that a change of moral direction is possible without any specific religious worldview. But the deeper question applies to the culture at large. Is it possible, or likely, that there is a broad "reformation of manners," as mentioned in the introduction, with the twofold goals of the English MP William Wilberforce? By "manners" he did not mean etiquette but rather morality. It is no accident that some of the most profound movements of social reform followed the religious revivals known as the Great Awakenings in the eighteenth and nineteenth centuries.

Sociologist James Davison Hunter expresses skepticism that such a moral reformation is possible without the resources religious communities provide. He describes the efforts of the culture to cultivate virtue without those resources: "While we desperately want the flower of morality to bloom and multiply, we have, at the same time, pulled the plant up out from the soil that sustains it."[11] Though Hunter does not hold that character requires religious faith, character does require "the conviction of *truth made sacred*, abiding as an authoritative presence within consciousness and life, reinforced by habits institutionalized within a moral community" and as part of "a story about living for a purpose that is bigger than oneself," so that people "come to understand not only how to be good but why."[12] Truth made sacred thus gives virtue its "commanding character and thus the power to inspire and shame."[13] This underscores how important it is to have morality within the framework of the sacred. Ultimately, a Christian worldview provides such a framework for morality to be compelling.

CHAPTER 4

What Does It Mean to Be Human?

So far we have seen that there is a moral crisis in American life — that we are in an ethical mess — and that part of the reason for that is the incoherent way in which we in our culture think about morality. We have established that there is a moral law that can be known and that it is possible to live a life of virtue. We have also seen that a Christian worldview provides resources for this pursuit of virtue that the culture simply does not have, thus making sense of both the view of morality and the journey to live it out.

In this chapter, we leave the realm of moral theory and put "shoe leather" on what we believe about right and wrong. Here we take up the complex world of bioethics — the application of morality to matters of life and death. The reason for this is twofold — issues of life and death are the most foundational of all, and they have the most serious and far-reaching consequences. We are asking several clear and straightforward questions: Who is included in the human community? What does it mean to be a human being? On what basis is life sacred? When does human personhood begin and end? Once we settle these questions, the specific issues surrounding abortion, assisted suicide, and eugenics come into clearer focus.

As a field surgeon on the battlefield, Dr. Ken Swan faced these questions as he operated on critically injured soldiers. On one particular day, Dr. Swan was the surgeon of the day, sitting in a back room having coffee with the nurses. Suddenly a nurse came running in and informed him that a badly injured soldier had just arrived. They brought him in on a stretcher, and Dr. Swan could see he was catastrophically injured.

Dr. Swan tells the story: "'How you doing, Ken?' His name was the same as mine, so I picked up on it, and he said, 'Well, I think I left my legs in the helicopter, Doc.' I know I remember saying to myself and I know I wrote it down in a letter I sent to my wife, 'He might just as well have left them in the helicopter because they're no good.'"

Ken had lots of other wounds—his left eye, his fifth finger on one hand, and his right testicle were all injured. His elbows were also badly fractured. But his vital signs were intact and fairly normal. He needed to have both legs amputated. The doctors also discovered that what had gone in his eye was now inside his skull, so he needed a craniectomy to remove the debris from his brain. And he needed to have one of his eyes taken out. So there were four doctors—the urologist, the neurosurgeon, the orthopedic surgeon, and Dr. Swan, who simultaneously went to work.

At the time, no one suggested they ought not to do the surgical procedures necessary to save the soldier. After six hours of surgery, they had finished patching him up. After they had wrapped up the surgery, Dr. Swan's boss, the chief of professional services, put his arm around Dr. Swan and said, "Brother Kenneth, I think you should know that the boys think that maybe you should have let that fellow go last night." Dr. Swan realized that such a thought hadn't even crossed his mind at the time.

A few days later, having expected the soldier to have succumbed to his various injuries, Dr. Swan was surprised when he was informed by the chaplain's assistant that Kenny had actually made it home.

At that point, Dr. Swan's worst fears were materializing. He said, "I pictured him with mother and father and a farmhouse and a back room, blind and confined to bed. And probably cigarette ashes all over him, and a can of beer next to him or something like that, and I thought how hideous that was."

Chuck Colson wrote about Dr. Swan in one of his books, *How Now Shall We Live?* He had seen a television reunion between Dr. Swan and Ken McGarrity, when Dr. Swan visited McGarrity's home in Georgia and discovered that the man he had saved was living a full life, that he was married with children, though he had faced many struggles along the way.[1] Colson commented, "So, in my mind, he made the right decision, even though his commanding officer chastised him for it. Even though Dr. Swan would tell you to this day he had doubts about whether or not he did the right thing."

Questions about the meaning and significance of being human are important because they are at the core of some of life's most fundamental questions. But they are also important because we live in a culture characterized by an erosion of respect for essential human dignity, by a coarsening of respect for life, particularly at the margins — at both the beginning and the end of life. Professor Robert George insists, "At the foundation of our thinking about ethics is the basic principle that every human being, regardless of how rich or poor, intelligent or not so intelligent, robust and healthy or severely debilitated, possesses a profound inherent and equal dignity and a right to life. So we must never suppose that there are some lives unworthy of being lived, that there are lives unworthy of life, that there are useless eaters, that there are people who are better off dead." This is the long-standing tradition of the sanctity of life — that life has intrinsic value and everyone possesses equal dignity, which is the basis of equal rights.

Abortion

I'll start the examples of the erosion of respect for life with the most obvious — abortion. Despite the cultural mantra that abortion be "safe, legal, and rare," today it is mostly safe, entirely legal from conception to birth, and *anything but rare*. Roughly a million (some estimate as many as 1.5 million) abortions are performed annually in the United States, and the figure has been steady since the 1973 Supreme Court decision, *Roe v. Wade*, that legalized abortion on demand for virtually any reason.[2] And for the foreseeable future, there does not seem to be any reasonable hope of the court overturning *Roe v. Wade*. Even if there were, it would leave the matter to the states to decide their own laws, and chances are that most states would immediately pass laws to keep abortion legal in their states. The law is no closer to protecting the sanctity of the life of the unborn than at any time since 1973.

At the grassroots level, progress is being made to discourage abortion and abortion providers. For example, some states have passed laws limiting partial-birth abortions, others require a waiting period before an abortion can be performed, and some even require counseling regarding alternatives to abortion. It is true that the number of abortion providers has dropped significantly in the last twenty years, particularly in smaller and more rural communities. In addition, with the advent of sophisticated ultrasound technology that enables physicians and expectant parents to look into the womb with much more detail than previously, public opinion is shifting more in favor of the unborn. It is increasingly difficult to hold the long-standing pro-choice view that the unborn is merely a clump of cells or a piece of tissue that is a part of the woman's body. Evidence of this progress comes from a *Time* magazine cover story (January 14, 2013) marking the fortieth anniversary of *Roe v. Wade*, which carried the provocative title "40 Years Ago, Abortion-Rights Activists Won an Epic Victory with *Roe v. Wade* — They've Been Losing Ever Since."

The conclusions of Kate Pickert, the story's author, about who's winning the battle may be overstated, though. In metropolitan areas, there is still broad access to abortion services, and in many states, taxpayers' dollars are used to fund abortions for poor women. The debate over abortion has also taken an ominous turn in recent years. Today many advocates of liberal abortion rights actually concede that the unborn child is a full human person with rights to be protected, yet also argue that the mother should have the right to end the life of her full-person unborn child. As early as 1971, philosopher Judith Jarvis Thomson tried to make the case that, even if the unborn child is a person, he or she does not have the right to the aid of the mother.[3] That is, the mother could cut off her aid to the child by abortion, and she would not have done anything wrong. Thomson used the following analogy to make her point:

> You wake up in the morning and find yourself back to back in bed with an unconscious violinist—a famous unconscious violinist. He has been found to have a fatal kidney ailment, and the Society of Music Lovers has canvassed all the available medical records and found that you alone have the right blood type to help. They have therefore kidnapped you, and last night the violinist's circulatory system was plugged into yours, so that your kidneys can be used to extract poisons from his blood as well as your own. The director of the hospital now tells you, "Look, we're sorry the Society of Music Lovers did this to you—we would never have permitted it if we had known. But still, they did it, and the violinist is now plugged into you. To unplug you would be to kill him. But never mind, it's only for nine months. By then he will have recovered from his ailment, and can safely be unplugged from you." Is it morally incumbent on you to accede to this situation? No doubt it would be very nice of you if you did, a great kindness. But do you have to accede to it? What if it were not nine months, but nine years? Or longer still? What if the director of the hospital says, "Tough luck. I agree. But now you've got to stay in bed, with the violinist plugged into you, for the rest of your

life. Because remember this: All persons have a right to life, and violinists are persons. Granted you have a right to decide what happens in and to your body, but a person's right to life outweighs your right to decide what happens in and to your body. So you cannot ever be unplugged from him." I imagine you would regard this as outrageous.[4]

Thomson argued that you are under no obligation to stay attached to the violinist, and the fact that he will die if you do not is irrelevant. Thus, she concluded, it is possible for the unborn child to be a full person yet for the mother to have the right over her own body such that abortion is permissible. Thomson was conceding the personhood of the unborn for the sake of her argument, though in 1971 not many feminists actually believed that about the unborn.

But roughly twenty-five years later, another feminist, pro-choice advocate, Naomi Wolf, made a similar concession about the unborn, with a different argument for abortion rights. Wolf argued that with advances in technology — namely ultrasound — it was becoming more difficult to make the case that an unborn child was merely a clump of cells, piece of tissue, or some other part of the mother's body. She too conceded that an unborn child was a full-person human being and made the argument that under the right circumstances, women still had the right to take the lives of their unborn children.

Since abortion became legal nearly a quarter-century ago, the fields of embryology and perinatology have been revolutionized — but the pro-choice view of the contested fetus has remained static. This has led to a bizarre bifurcation in the way we who are pro-choice tend to think about wanted as opposed to unwanted fetuses: the unwanted ones are still seen in schematic black-and-white drawings while the wanted ones have metamorphosed into vivid and moving color. Even while [then Surgeon General Jocelyn] Elders spoke of our need to "get over" our love affair with the unwelcome fetus, an entire growth industry — Mozart for your belly; framed sonogram photos; home fetal-heartbeat stethoscopes—is devoted to sparking fetal love affairs in other circumstances, and aimed especially at the hearts of overscheduled yuppies.

Any happy couple with a wanted pregnancy and a copy of *What to Expect When You're Expecting* can see the cute, detailed drawings of the fetus whom the book's owner presumably is not going to abort, and can read the excited descriptions of what that fetus can do and feel, month by month. Anyone who has had a sonogram during pregnancy knows perfectly well that the four-month-old fetus responds to outside stimulus—"Let's get him to look this way," the technician will say, poking gently at the belly of a delighted mother-to-be. *The Well Baby Book*, the kind of whole-grain holistic guide to pregnancy and childbirth that would find its audience among the very demographic that is most solidly pro-choice, reminds us that: "Increasing knowledge is increasing the awe and respect we have for the unborn baby and is causing us to regard the unborn baby as a real person long before birth."

So, what will it be: Wanted fetuses are charming, complex REM-dreaming little beings whose profile on the sonogram looks just like Daddy, but unwanted ones are mere "uterine material"? How can we charge that it is vile and repulsive for pro-lifers to brandish vile and repulsive images if the images are real? To insist that the truth is in poor taste is the very height of hypocrisy. Besides, if these images are often the facts of the matter, and if we then claim that it is offensive for pro-choice women to be confronted by them, then we are making the judgment that women are too inherently weak to face a truth about which they have to make a grave decision.[5]

Wolf goes on to describe this grave, moral decision:

It was when I was four months pregnant, sick as a dog, and in the middle of an argument, that I realized I could no longer tolerate the fetus-is-nothing paradigm of the pro-choice movement. I was being interrogated by a conservative, and the subject of abortion rights came up. "You're four months pregnant," he said. "Are you going to tell me that's not a baby you're carrying?" Had I not been so nauseated and so cranky and so weighed down with the physical gravity of what was going on inside me, I might not have told what is the truth for me. "Of course it's a baby," I snapped. And went rashly on: "And if I found myself in circumstances in which I had to make the terrible decision to end this life, then that would be between myself and God."[6]

Wolf was pleading for her feminist colleagues to recognize what technology, particularly today's 4-D ultrasound, is making more obvious — that the unborn cannot be seen as simply "uterine material." But what makes her view and others like it so alarming is *the admission that women still should have the right to take the life of their full-person unborn child.* Thankfully, Wolf admits that the abortion decision is indeed a moral one and one to be taken very seriously by women considering it. And she rightly recognizes that technology is surely making it harder to maintain the case that the unborn is only a part of the mother's body. But for some time the conventional wisdom was that once the personhood of the unborn was established, the debate was over, since the life of the unborn was seen to be of higher value than the mother's right over her body. That is, the right to life trumped the right over one's own body. Today that is no longer true. What makes the agenda of Wolf and others who advance a similar position so disturbing is that they can admit the unborn is a full person and still hold that women have the right to an abortion. You can see how this is evidence of erosion of respect for life at the margins.

Wolf is certainly right about the impact of technology on the abortion discussion, though certainly not everyone has come to the place Wolf has about the unborn. Technology has amplified a profound ambivalence in the culture today about the nature of the unborn. As an example of that ambivalence, take the widely publicized murder case of Laci Peterson by her husband Scott. He was convicted of murdering her on Christmas Eve 2002, when she was eight months pregnant. Both she and her unborn child were found when they washed ashore in San Francisco Bay. Scott Peterson was convicted for *two murders*, not one, though it was first-degree murder for Laci and second-degree murder for their unborn child, Conner. But the law provides for murder charges in the deaths of both the mother and the unborn child in cases like this, even though, hypothetically, Laci could have been on her way to a perfectly legal, partial-birth abortion at the time she was killed. What seems to make the difference in the law is that *Conner Peterson was a wanted child, whereas the children who are aborted are unwanted.* But wantedness is, of course, a commentary on the mother, not the unborn child. It has nothing to do with determining the nature of the unborn child.

By extension, if women can divest themselves of responsibility for their unborn children simply by their decision to do so — by their *choice* — then why are men held to eighteen years of responsibility for children they did not want? Why is their choice less relevant than the woman's? I am not saying we should let deadbeat dads off the hook for their obligation to help care for their children; rather, I am pointing out the inconsistency in the law when *wantedness* determines the right to life of the unborn child. Philosopher Keith Pavlischek describes the 1998 case of Peter Wallis and Kellie Smith under what he calls "paternal responsibilities and abortion rights":

Peter Wallis and Kellie Smith met at work, fell in love, shared an apartment. She got pregnant. He got mad. They split up. She gave birth to a baby girl. Mr. Wallis is now suing Ms. Smith for becoming pregnant against his will, accusing her of "intentionally acquiring and misusing" his semen when they had sexual intercourse. It is not just a modern love story, for it has profound implications for law and public policy. Wallis claims that Smith promised to take birth control pills but then quit without telling him. Smith says she took the pills but became pregnant accidentally. He offered to marry her, but she refused, claiming, "I realized that he didn't love me." He then urged her to have an abortion, thereby, one suspects, confirming her intuition. She refused and gave birth. Mr. Wallis claims this forced him into a role he did not choose: fatherhood and the child support that goes with it.

Pavlischek concludes:

Given the current abortion regime, the sole just, non-sexist, equitable legal solution is to extend to men the right to opt out of parenthood currently only available to women.... I say, "given the current abortion regime," for the abortion license forces upon us such perverse consistency. We could hold fathers and mothers legally responsible for their sexual activity and for their children from the time they are conceived. But that, of course, would entail the legal protection of the unborn from harm, from the time they are conceived. Which is, after all, not such a bad idea.[7]

Further evidence of erosion of respect for life today includes things that would have been considered unthinkable not that long ago but are happening periodically today. For example, take the instances of teenagers giving birth at the prom, stuffing the baby in the trash, and returning to the dance. Or consider the number of babies abandoned just after birth in churches and other safe havens — an improvement from infanticide, granted, but disturbing nonetheless. A further example of what would have been unimaginable a few decades ago is the debate over the "born alive rule." This rule, adopted by law at the federal level, states that any baby born alive must be protected and cannot be the object of infanticide, even when the child is born as a result of a botched abortion. Before becoming law at the federal level, this was debated at many state levels — the very fact that such a rule even had to be debated and voted on struck many people as an outrageous erosion of respect for life.

But perhaps the most glaring example of what would have been unthinkable a generation ago is what was uncovered at the abortion clinic of Dr. Kermit Gosnell. In early 2011, Dr. Gosnell was indicted for eight murders — one woman who died under his malpractice and seven babies who were killed after being born alive in his clinic. A 261-page grand jury report revealed conditions in his downtown Philadelphia clinic that defied belief.

> Furniture and blankets were stained with blood. Instruments were not properly sterilized. Disposable medical supplies ... were reused, over and over again. Medical equipment ... was generally broken; even when it worked, it wasn't used. The emergency exit was padlocked shut. And scattered throughout, in cabinets, in the basement, in a freezer, in jars and bags and plastic jugs, were fetal remains. *It was a baby charnel house.*[8]
>
> The grand jury felt obligated to insist that 'Pennsylvania is not a third world country ... even nail salons in Pennsylvania are monitored more closely for client safety."[9]

Gosnell was indicted for seven cases of infanticide (he had destroyed enough evidence so that he was indicted for only seven cases), but as Joseph Bottum comments:

> Those cases are enough to sicken anyone. The baby he delivered alive at seven and a half months, for instance, and then snipped its spinal cord, packed it in a shoe box and joked that it was so big it could "walk me to the bus stop." And the 28-week-old fetus whose corpse was discovered in the clinic packed in a frozen water bottle. And the baby who lived for more than 20 minutes before an assistant finally came in and cut the spinal cord "just the way" the grand jury was told, "she had seen Gosnell do it so many times."[10]

The grand jury report alleges hundreds of cases like these. One clinic employee admitted to severing the spinal cords of roughly one hundred babies, each beyond twenty-four weeks of gestational age.

And Gosnell is not the only abortion provider who engaged in these troubling practices. Take the example of Abu Hayat, nick-named "the butcher of Avenue A" in New York City, who "killed a 17-year-old girl in a botched abortion and denied ever having her as a patient ... or the Florida clinic that delivered a baby at 23 weeks and threw it out alive, in a nearby garbage can ... or New Jersey's Stephen Brigham, who performed abortions in his van, driving them from state to state to skirt state laws against late-term abortions."[11]

In academic circles, the notion of infanticide has generated a new term to describe it euphemistically — "the after-birth abortion." Whereas in the past, support for these practices had come from extreme though respected figures in bioethics, such as Princeton professor Peter Singer and philosopher Michael Tooley, today more credibility is given to such positions, as their proponents recognize they are simply being consistent with their abortion justification logic. And more abortion advocates are comfortable with taking their pro-choice position to its logical conclusion — thereby justifying abortions after birth also. For example, in a highly regarded article in the well-respected *Journal of Medical Ethics*, the authors argue that what "we call 'after-birth abortion' *should be permissible in all cases where abortion is, including cases where the newborn is not disabled.*"[12] If human beings do not have intrinsic dignity from conception forward, then the ability to perform certain elementary functions, such as self-awareness or awareness of one's environment, is what determines when a person is worthy of protection. So even Peter Singer's limit of the first thirty days after birth for justifiable infanticide is arbitrary and could conceivably and consistently be extended for the first twelve to eighteen months after birth.

EMBRYO/STEM CELL RESEARCH

Not only are the unborn (and newborns) being denied their intrinsic dignity, but human embryos are as well. These embryos are widely regarded as merely "clumps of cells" or "bags of marbles" and thus have no value other than what other human beings assign to them based on their utilitarian usefulness. For the first time in our history, we are sacrificing the lives of human beings in embryonic form in order to benefit others — that is, we are harvesting the stem cells from human embryos to benefit patients with a variety of diseases. For now, the process of harvesting stem cells kills the embryo, and to date, thousands of embryos have been destroyed in the process of harvesting their stem cells.

In addition, over four hundred thousand embryos are presently *in storage* in infertility clinics across the United States. That means there are as many children in embryonic form in cold storage in these clinics who have been conceived through in vitro fertilization (IVF) — a very common infertility treatment in which conception takes place in the lab instead of in the body. Though it is common to regard these embryos as a sack of cells, ask any couple who has had children through IVF, and they will likely tell you that they know intuitively that those embryos in storage are more than clumps of cells — they can trace the origins of their children back to the embryonic state. Professor Robert George says:

> The first thing I think that we have to be clear about is that a human embryo is in fact, a human being. A human being at a very early stage of development, but it's not a nonhuman creature or a subhuman creature. Each of us who is today an adult was at an earlier stage in his or her life an adolescent, and before that a child, and before that a newborn infant, and before that a fetus, and before that an embryo. These terms don't name different things or different kinds of things; rather, they name the same kind of thing, and indeed the same thing that is a human being at different stages of development.

Advocates of using human embryos for research often use the analogy of the "fire in the infertility clinic" to attempt to argue for their position that embryos do not have the moral status of persons. They ask, if you were walking with your two-year-old child in an infertility clinic in which you had embryos in storage and a fire broke out and you only had time to save your two-year-old or your embryos, who would you save? They ask that as a rhetorical question because they think the answer is obvious — you would save your two-year-old. They then conclude that you can't possibly believe your embryos and your two-year-old have the same moral status. Thus it must be permissible to use embryos for research purposes even if it means destroying them.

But if you think about that analogy a bit, you'll see that the conclusion doesn't follow from who you would save from the fire. If you change the characters around, the choice is not quite as clear. If my choice were between saving my embryos and a serial rapist, I would save the embryos. But does that mean the rapist has less moral status than my embryos? Not necessarily. It only means that the emotional connection illustrated by the decision about whom to save has little to do with someone's moral status and dignity. For example, I would grieve much more if my dog were run over by a car than I would if a child in the Middle East were killed by a suicide bomber. The reason is that I have an emotional connection to my dog that I don't have to a child halfway around the world. Does that mean my dog has greater moral status and dignity than the child on the other side of the world? Of course not. The emotional attachment to and the moral status of the individual in question are unrelated, and who I would save from the clinic fire does not determine who has greater moral status.

Physician-Assisted Suicide/Euthanasia

As we consider the other end of life, it has been a long time since then governor of Colorado Richard Lamm's 1984 statement that the elderly "have a duty to die and get out of the way."[13] But since that time, four states — Washington, Oregon, Montana, and Vermont — have legalized physician-assisted suicide (PAS), with several more likely to follow. Though assisted suicide remains illegal in most states and euthanasia is illegal in all states (the difference being that in euthanasia the physician actually administers the lethal medication, whereas in PAS, the patient administers it with the aid of the physician), anecdotal evidence suggests that both do occur, though the regularity with which it happens is hard to establish since there is rarely any reporting of such incidents.

In Europe there is little distinction between assisted suicide and euthanasia — both are legal in some countries (the Netherlands and Belgium, for example) — and in other European countries the laws prohibiting such practices are more loosely enforced.[14] Studies of physicians' self-reporting that have come out of the Netherlands indicate that roughly 15 percent of euthanasia cases are performed without the explicit consent of the patient and usually without his or her knowledge. The Dutch coined a term for this practice some time ago — crypthanasia, or euthanasia done cryptically.

One current example of the trend toward euthanasia in Europe occurred in Belgium, where euthanasia is legal and generally performed in cases of terminal illness and/or suffering that cannot be alleviated. In this case, however, forty-five-year-old twin brothers who were born deaf and were in the process of going blind chose euthanasia as opposed to the prospect of being institutionalized. What makes this case unusual is that neither of the twins was terminally ill or suffering pain that could not be alleviated. Claiming they had nothing to live for, they opted for ending their lives.[15]

In many countries where the possibility of PAS/euthanasia exists, the elderly have become one of the most vulnerable groups in society. Not only are they victimized by elder abuse, a growing phenomena, but as health care costs continue to rise and the elderly become a growing part of the population, the pressure to provide less care at the end of life for the elderly will likely increase. That may include greater pressure to legalize physician-assisted suicide in more states and further "warehousing" of the aged who cannot care for themselves any longer.

EUGENICS

Further evidence of the coarsening of respect for the intrinsic dignity of life comes in the field of genetics and reproductive technology. As Mayo Clinic physician Dr. Chris Hook suggests, eugenics (a Greek word literally translated "well born") has returned.

> The eugenics movement did not go away. It really changed how it expressed itself. With the explosion of genetic information through the human genome project, the use of that information for reproductive choice—that's not just necessarily to abort or to not implant embryos, but whether or not to conceive children in the first place—is going to be used.
>
> There has been the use of preimplantation genetic diagnosis to allow certain normal individuals to live while other normal embryos were discarded. I'll give you an example. In 2001 there was a case of a ... little girl who had an inherited bone marrow problem called "Fanconi's anemia." The best way to cure this was through a matched sibling bone marrow transplant. You could get it from a nonsibling donor, but there would be other immunologic consequences and elements of that. So her parents ... conceived roughly thirty embryos through in vitro fertilization. They first checked them for the presence or absence of the Fanconi's anemia gene then discarded those that had the defect. They then did testing to see if the embryos were going to be a perfect match for the young girl. Even though they were normal, if they weren't a match, they were discarded. That left four, and they did single embryo transfers, and ultimately a brother was born who served as a bone marrow donor.
>
> Now, in one sense, one can certainly understand the desires of a parent to do what they could to save their child. But as I think about what might happen in the mind of the young boy at some point, when he asks, "Well Mom and Dad, tell me how I came to be." If they're honest and they explain the whole situation, he is going to sit back and say, "Now, wait a minute. There were these other nor-

mal embryos, but you threw them away and you kept me because I could serve as my sister's bone marrow donor (which is a problem as well)." So, eugenics is very much alive and well; it's just being expressed in different ways.

Eugenics certainly got a bad name as a result of its association with the Nazis during World War II. But it did not originate with them. It became popular around the turn of the twentieth century among the intellectual elite in the United States and Europe. One of the first and most public proponents of eugenics was Margaret Sanger, founder of Planned Parenthood. And in 1927 the US Supreme Court held that forced sterilization of the mentally disabled and habitually criminal was not a violation of the Constitution (later overturned in 1942). Justice Oliver Wendell Holmes summarized the court's view with his famous statement that "three generations of imbeciles is enough."[16]

One of the dangers of eugenics is the impact on how society views and values people with disabilities. It affects how we see people who have genetic abnormalities and often results in people with physical or mental challenges being devalued. Joni Eareckson Tada reflects on our culture's values in contrast to biblical values:

When I first became spinal cord injured and realized my quadriplegia was total and permanent, at first I didn't want to live. I think that's because, back then, I was way too influenced by the things that society values, like appearance, abilities, whether or not I could contribute, whether or not I could walk or run.

Yet, even though I could not use my hands or legs, I was still the same person, I was still me. My instinctive desire to live far outweighed my despair. That's when I began to look into the Bible. I had to understand why I still prized my life. The Bible showed me that it centered on my being created by a God of intent and compassion. This wasn't any accident; this was planned. My dignity as a human being was directly linked to God. Society may say that it extols human dignity, but it does not; it cannot. When you take that out of the picture, we are not even glorified animals. That spells bad news for people with disabilities.

Quadriplegics like me have never fared well in societies that view life as dispensable. When society attaches life value to how a person functions, or what they can contribute or do, then people with severe disabilities, the elderly, or anyone who is weak, their lives are at risk. Not only must life not be destroyed, it must be honored. The way we treat those who are weak is a reflection of what we value. If we prize the God of all creation, we will value the life he has made.

Dr. Hook mentioned that the eugenics movement is expressing itself in subtler ways today. Take genetic testing, for example, particularly when done on unborn children in the womb. Benefits of prenatal genetic testing include being able to detect a wide variety of genetic abnormalities, thus enabling couples to be prepared for having a child with physical or mental challenges. But many couples who get bad news back from a genetic test use the information to end the pregnancy. In fact, the vast majority of pregnancies in which genetic testing reveals an anomaly are terminated, which is somewhat ironic, given our culture's heightened sensitivity to diversity. What illustrates the coarsening of respect for life is the assumption that underlies the decisions to end these pregnancies — that is, that the child with the genetic abnormality has a life not worth living. This comes from the further presumption that there is a necessary connection between disability and unhappiness. But that's clearly not true. It would be very interesting to take an informal poll of children with some of these challenges and ask them if they think they would have been better off never having been born. I suspect they would be quite puzzled, if not insulted, by the question, and rightly so.

Chuck Colson is one of those people who would have been offended by such a question. He said:

This issue is very personal to some of us. I have a nineteen-year-old autistic grandson, who if Dr. Peter Singer here at

Princeton, who believes in the utilitarian calculus for determining who lives and who dies, had his way, would have been killed the moment he was born (or aborted prior to birth). I take it very personally because I've seen how Max, my grandson, has affected the lives of thousands of people. He is a great blessing. He has transformed our whole family. He has taught us about love on a whole new dimension.

Perhaps even subtler is the way genetic testing has changed the burden of proof in decisions about ending a pregnancy. When a couple with a normal pregnancy decide to end it, we usually think of the burden of justification being on them to provide a compelling reason for termination. The default position is that you would keep a healthy pregnancy. But once there is bad news from a genetic test, the burden of proof shifts. The default position is now that the couple will end the pregnancy, and the burden of justification is on the couple who wants to continue the pregnancy. My neighbors have a child with Down syndrome, and it was very interesting to hear them tell of their experience with the decision to continue the pregnancy. It was assumed they would end the pregnancy, and they received subtle pressure to be really sure they wanted to keep the child. And I've heard others describe the way they think when they see parents with children who have disabilities — they sometimes catch themselves judgmentally thinking, "Don't you know you didn't have to have that child?"

Other indications that eugenics are back include the growing emphasis on gender selection, particularly now that the technology exists to select the sex of your child without having to undergo surgical abortion. Embryos created through IVF can be screened through what Dr. Hook referred to above as "preimplantation genetic diagnosis" (PGD), and the embryos that are of the desired gender are then implanted and the rest discarded. In addition, you can select the sex of your child prior to conception with "Micro-Sort," a sperm separating technology that provides an 85 percent likelihood of obtaining your desired gender.

In the developing world, however, the more traditional methods of sex selection — abortion, infanticide, and abandonment — are used. A 2010 cover article in *The Economist* exposes a "war on baby girls," also known as "gendercide," in the developing world. Their sources estimate that over 100 million baby girls have been aborted or killed or have otherwise disappeared in the past thirty years, and the number is rising.[17] This has made the gender gap between males and females around the world wider, a demographic trend that has social scientists worried.

Not only can couples select the sex of their child, but they can also select for traits, though not with the same high probability as with sex selection. Couples today can select the traits of sperm and egg donors from which they can choose to conceive their child. Eggs and sperm with these desired traits are for sale on the open market, as numerous infertility clinics and their associated websites attest. Female college students are routinely solicited by ads in their campus newspapers to be egg donors. Some ads offer as much as $75,000 for a harvest of eggs if the women meet certain criteria. In one case, the donor woman must be five feet ten inches tall or taller, athletic, blonde, blue-eyed, and she must have scored over 1400 on the SAT exam. Not only can couples select so-called desirable traits, but they can also select *for* disability. For example, a British same-sex couple, both of whom were deaf, sought out a deaf sperm donor in order to conceive a deaf child. They succeeded. Though the case generated a great deal of discussion and a lot of criticism of the couple, it was very interesting to see how difficult it was to articulate any critique of the couple in the culture of relativism (where people make up their own moral rules for themselves) described in chapter 2.[18]

What Does It Mean to Be Human?

So how do we begin to answer the question raised at the beginning of this chapter: What does it mean to be human? Or to put it another way, who is a member of the human community, and on what basis? And the practical question: How does that affect decisions about abortion, embryonic stem cell research and treatments, euthanasia, and eugenics?

We can sharpen the question so we don't get confused in the midst of a complicated discussion: What does it mean to be a *person*? The designation of a "person" has less to do with science and more to do with a being's moral status, implying rights and protections that follow from being a person. For most of the history of civilization, it was assumed that a human being and a person were the same thing — that all human beings were also persons. It is true that there were some exceptions to this — slaves, for example, were historically considered human beings but were not recognized as having the rights of persons. In some cultures, this was also how women were regarded. This was also the way Jews were viewed in Nazi Germany — human beings to be sure, but not having the moral status of persons.

A further point of clarification is that what constitutes a human being may be a scientific set of categories, but what constitutes a person has nothing to do with science and everything to do with philosophy. Science cannot tell us what a person is, because personhood is not a scientific question but a philosophical one. What science can tell us is what a human being is — that from conception forward, the union of egg and sperm is a living and separate entity with its own unique genetic code (except in the case of identical twins). In addition, it is fully human if it has the characteristically human genetic code. Think about it like this: if embryos were neither living nor human, then researchers and health clinics would not be nearly so interested in their stem cells. Science is clear that from conception onward, a living human being exists. Of course, embryos are not fully mature human beings. But neither are postviability fetuses or newborns or toddlers or preschoolers. But from the moment of conception, the embryo has all it needs to mature — if given nutrients and shelter that the womb normally provides. I suggest being careful about how we talk about embryos so that we don't inadvertently betray our view. Embryos don't *become* fetuses; fetuses don't *become* newborns. Nor do embryos *develop* into fetuses and fetuses into newborns. This type of language suggests that in the process they actually become something different than they already are. But that's not true. Embryos *mature* into fetuses, which *mature* into newborns, which *mature* into toddlers, and so on.

Yet science can take us only so far in this discussion of what constitutes a person. This is a very important point to make, since in the culture, science is routinely regarded as the only source of real knowledge about the world. Remember how in chapter 2 I argued that morality constituted things that we could know? I recognized a distinction between knowledge and belief, and pointed out that culturally knowledge was reserved for the realm of science while everything else was relegated to the realm of belief or opinion. That discussion of morality as something that can be *known* is crucial, because here's another area that is equally important — what constitutes a person. If that's simply a matter of belief or opinion, then human rights are in serious jeopardy, because they rest on subjective belief, which is ever changing and hardly a secure basis for something as important as basic rights. In addition, it is crucial to see these rights as being *recognized* not *conferred*. Today rights are commonly seen as being granted by the government to individuals. But what government grants, government can also take away, and the history of the twentieth century is the story of what happens to human rights when government gives and takes them away. This is why the American founders were so insistent that these rights, including the right to life, were *endowed by our Creator*, and that they were what they called "inalienable," meaning they could not be forfeited or otherwise taken away without due process of law.

So what constitutes a person is not fundamentally a scientific question but a philosophical one. I made this point in a debate years ago with a biologist and an embryonic stem cell harvesting advocate, and to his credit, the scientist actually conceded my point that science can't definitively answer what is essentially a philosophical question. I nearly fell out of my chair when I heard him say that! But where the discussion went from there was not so encouraging. He claimed that if science can't answer the question, then it is a matter of opinion, and one person's opinion is as good as the next, reducing it to subjective belief. He was still stuck in the worldview that science was the only area of real knowledge and that the rest was belief. I suggested that the categories of knowledge were broader than he thought, that philosophical reason and argument could also produce knowledge. I argued that the philosophers on his campus might be surprised to hear that their views did not contribute to the advancement of real knowledge!

This debate about the use of embryonic stem cells actually provided an ideal setting to articulate an answer to this question of what constitutes a person and who belongs in the human community. I was debating this in a health care community consisting of physicians, nurses, administrators, board members, research scientists, and community members. They came from a very diverse set of backgrounds and worldviews. As a result, I couldn't rush in with my theologically grounded views and argue that if human beings are not made in God's image, then human dignity and human rights are both oxymorons. They would have concluded that my religious views, if they didn't share them (and they probably didn't), would have no relevance to forming their views on the subject. But views on the subject at hand that I was representing (embryonic stem cell research) were too important to be so easily dismissed. I wasn't willing to give people such an easy way out from having to consider that embryos are persons too, with dignity and rights. So I attempted to formulate this argument in a format not exclusively dependent on my Christian worldview. Of course, it was consistent with my Christian view of the world but not entirely reliant on it. This turned out to be a wise strategy, because one of the health system's board members unloaded on me in the question and answer session with the remark, "I'm so tired of you religious people imposing your moral views on the rest of us!" I replied, as graciously as I could, "Let's get rid of this silly notion that it's only religious people who are imposing their views on the culture. All law is the imposition of somebody's morality. You are also imposing a moral view on the rest of us — that an embryo is not a person and can be destroyed for the benefit of others." And since we had already settled that science could not provide a determinative answer to our issue, he could not appeal to that. I also challenged him to point out any places where I had invoked the Bible or theology in my presentation, which he couldn't because I hadn't. We didn't hear from this board member for the rest of the evening!

When it came time to present my views on embryonic stem cell research, I had the opportunity to make the case that all human beings from conception forward ought to count as members of the human community, be recognized as persons, and be given the right to life. I began with our commonsense view of what constitutes a person — that the notion of personhood is something we are, not something we do. I pointed out that we recognize there is something fundamental about persons that enables them to have the same identity through time and change. Philosophers call this a "substance" view of a person, that our continuity of personal identity through time and change is grounded in an immaterial essence, which for centuries people have called a soul. This is also known as an *essential* view of a person, or what other philosophers call an *endowment* view of a person.[19]

What makes this our commonsense view of a person comes from the way we view moral responsibility and criminal justice. Take the latter of these. If someone commits a crime and it takes years to capture the person and bring him or her to justice, we presume the person standing before the court is the same person who committed the crime (assuming it is not a case of mistaken identity). If the person argued that he or she had undergone physical changes, such as loss of hair, cosmetic surgery, even amputation, and as a result, was not the same person who had committed the crime, that person would likely be laughed out of court, and justifiably so. The reason is that the court operates on a substance view of a person — that there is a continuity of personal identity that endures through time and change. But if human persons are nothing more than a collection of physical parts and properties, then there is no adequate basis for recognizing this continuity of identity. In fact, the person in court could argue that he or she has undergone significant changes, such as recycling through all their cells (which we all do every seven years) and make a plausible case that they are not the same entity that committed the crime. But our intuition about persons tells us something different — that persons are what they are, not what they do. There is a difference between *being a person* and *functioning as a person*.

Here's another way to think about this, again based on our commonsense view of a human being. Every human person is the result of a continual process of growth and development that begins at conception — not much debate about that, though I would use the term *maturity* instead of *development* here. Further, and admittedly more controversial, *there is no morally or ontologically relevant break in the process from conception to birth. Ontological* refers to the notion of being — what kind of a thing is the person? That is, what point in the pregnancy makes a difference in terms of what kind of a thing the unborn child is? What I mean is that there is no decisive moment during pregnancy at which you can clearly say you have a person, whereas one day before you did not. All points along the continuum from conception to birth are arbitrary points of delineation that have no necessary connection to the moral and ontological status of a person. Take, for example, birth as the decisive moment recognized by the law. But what exactly is the difference between an unborn child one day before birth and a newborn child one day after birth? Other than a change of location, which is not relevant to the child's moral status, and a slight change in the degree of dependence on the mother, there is virtually no difference.

Interestingly, in the bioethics community, there is increasing recognition of the irrelevance of birth as a marker for personhood, as the defenders of "after-birth abortion" and infanticide point out. Implantation as a decisive moment suffers from the same problem — whether an embryo is in the lab or in the womb, it is just changing location. And it doesn't really matter that the lab is not a suitable location for an embryo to flourish. If I sent a group of my students to the moon, even though that's not an environment where they are able to survive and thrive, that has nothing to do with their status as persons. It is merely a change in location with an additional qualifier that constitutes a distinction without a difference.

Viability, the ability of a child to survive outside the womb, is another good example of a commonly held decisive moment. Though it varies from child to child, it occurs at roughly twenty-four to twenty-six weeks of pregnancy. For several years, the conventional wisdom in the culture was that abortion was legal up until viability and restricted after that. The reason for that view was that when *Roe v. Wade* was decided in 1973, viability was at the end of the second trimester, and the Supreme Court held that in the third trimester, the state had a legitimate interest in the protection of fetal life. The exceptions to this, in effect, make abortion legal through the third trimester too. But today, through advances in medical technology, viability has been moved back into the second trimester. And that is what viability actually measures — the state of prenatal medical technology. Viability is irrelevant to the ontological status of the unborn, and the fact that it is so variable from baby to baby renders it even more suspect as an indicator of the status of the unborn. Further, think about what viability actually indicates about the ability of the unborn child to survive outside the womb. A baby born at twenty-four to twenty-six weeks is not like a full-term newborn who goes into the mother's arms as soon as the umbilical cord is cut and breathes on her own. Premature babies born at the point of viability go from the natural life-support system of the mother to an artificial life-support system in the neonatal intensive care unit (NICU). That is, they exchange natural life support for an artificial one and remain on it until they mature sufficiently to be weaned off of it, usually as close to the full term of pregnancy as possible.

We can make a similar argument about any point in the pregnancy at which personhood is proposed, that the decisive moment makes no necessary commentary on the status of the unborn and thus cannot be a criteria for determining when there is a person. So take the two premises set forth so far — that all adult persons are the result of a continuous process of development (maturity) that begins at conception and that there is no morally or ontologically relevant break in the process from conception to birth. If those two premises are true, then the conclusion that follows is that a person exists from conception forward. The way I would put this to a skeptical friend or coworker is to ask them, "If the unborn child is not a person at conception, at what point do you think it becomes one?"

Some will agree that these decisive moments are not so decisive when it comes to what constitutes a person. But they use a different set of criteria to determine when a person exists. They argue that the indicators of personhood include things like self-consciousness, self-awareness, awareness of one's environment, sentience (the ability to experience sensations such as pain), and some capacity for relationships. This is often expressed in a popular way by what is called "the look in the mirror test" — the ability to recognize oneself as oneself when looking in the mirror. This is what is often called a functional view of a person, that the designation of a person can only be made when he or she is able to perform certain critical functions such as the ones just mentioned. On a functional view, the unborn, the seriously mentally impaired, those in a vegetative state, and others would be human beings but not persons and would not have the rights of persons. Most who hold to after-birth abortion/infanticide base it on some sort of functional view of a person.

This functional view of a person suffers from at least two significant shortcomings. First, there are times in most of our lives when we don't meet the functional criteria for being a person. Take someone who is in a reversible coma or, more commonly, who is under general anesthesia. If the anesthesia is working properly, the person has lost all functional criteria, albeit temporarily. But as soon as you make the counterargument that it's temporary, you have admitted that during that temporary time period, there is something else besides those functions that grounds that person's status and corresponding rights. Since the person doesn't have those functions, what keeps him or her a person sounds a lot like an essence I discussed earlier in this chapter.

A further weakness of this view is that it leads to a very counterintuitive notion that being a person is a matter of degree, what philosophers call a "degreed property." That is, it is something you can have more or less of as opposed to an all-or-nothing property. If personhood is based on these functions you can have more or less ability to perform, then personhood is degreed, and so are the rights and protectability of the person. For example, a person in a vegetative state or at the end of a terminal illness who has a lower level of functioning would have fewer rights to life, and thus laws authorizing removing of treatments from them or actually putting them to death, with or without their consent, would be plausible. And that's the rub — you can't have personhood being *degreed* and have *equal* rights at the same time. The only way to adequately ground equal rights is for every human being to have equal dignity and to recognize the difference between being a person and functioning as a person — that is, to recognize that a person is something you are, not something you do. You function as a person because you are one, not vice versa. To have a robust commitment to equal rights, it is critical to safeguard the inherent dignity of all human beings regardless of their ability to perform certain functions deemed critical for persons to perform.

CONCLUSION

This view of a human person that maintains the sanctity of life from conception forward is consistent with a Christian worldview, which is clear that there is no distinction between a human being and a person, and grounds dignity for all in the essential quality of being made in God's image. If human beings are not made in God's image, then human dignity is at worst an oxymoron and at best simply a human creation that can be taken away as easily as it can be bestowed. And it is government that usually both bestows and takes it away, and the dismal history of human rights in many parts of the world during the past century shows what life can be like under such a view. The founders of the United States were clear that human rights were "endowed by our Creator" and recognized by government, not bestowed by the state. This is what is meant by the term "sanctity of life" — that all human beings are persons with intrinsic dignity and the right to life, regardless of their ability to function or their level of developmental maturity, from conception forward.

Pro-choice advocates, who concede this notion of the sanctity of life for the unborn and still support liberal abortion rights, are actually caught in a very knotty conceptual bind once they make that crucial concession. Far from the mother's right over her own body taking precedence over the life of the unborn child, as pro-choice advocates have argued, the conclusion that ought to be drawn from the sanctity of life of the unborn child is quite the opposite. If someone admits that in the womb a full-person unborn child is maturing, *then the unborn child actually has a claim on the mother's body for the resources he or she needs.*[20]

Think about it this way: Imagine you and your spouse have a six-month-old child, and that like many new parents, you are overwhelmed with caring for him, are constantly fatigued, and always seem to need a break. So the two of you decide you very much need a getaway, and you make plans for a two-week vacation to Hawaii. But instead of arranging for child care, you stockpile diapers and bottles of formula, pat your child on the head on your way out the door, and tell him you'll be back in two weeks. Upon your return, you will likely face a number of angry people awaiting your arrival, including neighbors, grandparents, the police, and child protective services representatives. The police will likely file charges against you for child endangerment and negligence, and should the child have died during your absence, you will be charged with negligent homicide.

Think about why those charges would be filed. Certainly one reason would be because you abandoned your responsibilities as parents. But with those responsibilities are the child's corresponding rights — the right to the resources of the parents necessary to survive and have an adequate start in life. If you were unfit parents, the responsibility for providing those resources would default to the community or the state. Or you might have transferred those responsibilities to another in adoption. A child has a claim on his or her parents for the resources needed to survive, so if the parents fail to provide them, the child has been wronged. If that's true of a six-month-old child, and we have conceded that an unborn child is a full person, then why wouldn't the unborn child have a similar claim on the mother's body for the resources he or she needs while in the womb? It would certainly seem that the unborn child in the womb would have such a claim.

Regarding the end of life, we need to be clear about what the sanctity of life does not mean. The right to life does not carry with it a corresponding responsibility to keep everyone alive at all times and at all costs. In a Christian worldview, with death as a conquered enemy, this means death need not always be resisted. If we hold that we must keep everyone alive no matter what, a view called "vitalism," then this seems to make the statement that earthly life is the highest good for human beings. But theologically that's not true. Earthly life is not the ultimate good; our eternal life with God is our highest good, and earthly life is what we call a penultimate good, meaning it is close to the top but not the ultimate.

Under the right conditions, it is consistent with the sanctity of life to say "enough" to medicine and allow a terminal disease to take its natural course. There is a significant moral difference between killing and allowing to die, and it is killing that is prohibited in Christian teaching. Allowing death to take its course when further treatment is futile or more burdensome than beneficial is consistent with the sanctity of life and avoids unnecessarily delaying someone's eternal homecoming. Of course, if the prognosis for the patient is good and there is a reasonable hope of recovery, then allowing him or her to die would be unconscionable. But where the prognosis is very poor and medicine cannot do much for the patient (or what doctors can do is so burdensome it outweighs the benefits), stopping treatment is acceptable. It is best when patients make these decisions for themselves, either orally or in writing, in an advance directive (sometimes knows as a "living will"), and families sometimes make these decisions. When they do, it is very important that they accurately represent the wishes of the patient.

These issues at the edges of life are critically important because they touch on the most basic of human rights — the right to life. A consistent ethic of life is based on the Judeo-Christian ideas of equal dignity before God because all people are made in God's image. Historian Glenn Sunshine says:

> When Christianity came along, they opposed abortion and infanticide, coming out of the Jewish tradition. The first legal appeal the early Christians made to the Roman government wasn't to stop persecution; it was to stop killing innocent babies. It was to stop infanticide and abortion as legal murder. What people don't understand is that the opposition to abortion and infanticide stems from precisely the same ideas that led the early Christians to oppose slavery, to promote women and the position of women in the communities, to support the general ideas that will emerge as the western tradition of human rights.

Professor Robert George summarizes it nicely when he says, "The basis of our ethics and at the base of our medicine, [was] the proposition that every human being has profound, inherent and equal dignity."

CHAPTER 5

Ethics in the Marketplace

Acursory reading of the news is all it takes to be aware of the corporate scandals that have occurred over the past decade or so and what the lack of ethics means in the business world. Eric Pillmore, a turnaround specialist who once described himself as a "corporate pooper scooper," was called in to help clean up the mess at Tyco in the early 2000s in the aftermath of a major scandal. He described his experience with the lack of ethics at Tyco:

> This was 2002 in the midst of ... Enron, WorldCom, and Tyco. The situation there was there was a CEO of the company who had charges brought against him related to his personal tax situation, which basically led to the uncovering by the board of directors of a major fraud, a theft of $600 million by the CFO and the CEO. I was part of the turnaround team brought in in the summer of 2002 to help investigate what had happened. Then, more importantly, look at what needed to change in order to get the company back on its feet and participate in trying to rebuild the integrity and reputation of financial markets in the US.

Really on three fronts I think things were pretty badly broken, both from a leadership standpoint, from a process point of a view, and then from a cultural standpoint inside the company. From a leadership standpoint, the company was led by a man by the name of Dennis Kozlowski, who was an autocratic, intimidating leader leading a company of 240,000 people, but leading it basically out of fear. He was able to take and build processes where there was no accountability to the CEO's office or the senior leadership team around him. He surrounded himself with people who could be easily influenced by his leadership style and would not push back at the right time. With his ability to bring the types of people in, create processes with no accountability, and then lead via this process, he basically built blind ambition into the minds of the people and sought what I call selfish ambition. We always say it's lonely at the top. Well, it is. There is a real emptiness. The dream is if I can just achieve this much more, I'll fill that emptiness. We all know that's not true. But the psychology of the individual at the time, I think, particularly at these heady times in the late '90s and the early part of this decade, [2000–2009] folks pursued that, pursued wealth at kind of any cost and without any regard for others. *It was more driven by selfish greed.*

What Pillmore faced at Tyco was an organizational culture that was not conducive to ethical behavior — just the opposite was modeled by the people at the top. Tyco was not the only company at that time dealing with ethical and legal scandals. Enron, WorldCom, Arthur Andersen, and many others were involved in accounting improprieties in the late 1990s and early 2000s. And as Ben Stein described in chapter 1, numerous Wall Street banks acted unethically, prompting the financial crisis of 2008–2009. Public cynicism about business is widely held today — just look at the number of movies and television programs in which the villain is a corporate executive. Today the most common antihero in popular culture and media is the CEO of a large corporation. Make a list of some of the movies you've seen in the last year and see how many have a CEO as the bad guy.

Be careful to put this public cynicism about business in perspective, however. Remember that the companies that engage in scandalous behavior are the ones that make the news. The executives arrested in their offices and forced to make the "perp walk" to jail — those are the ones who get their pictures in the newspaper and appear on the evening news. There is nothing newsworthy about companies that do things right, follow the law, treat their employees well, and have a culture of trust in the organization. You might even say they are somewhat boring! But they are also the majority of companies, though in some parts of the world that may not be true.

Think about the millions of transactions conducted every day that are premised on trust. It's not greed but trust that is the engine of a flourishing economy. A properly functioning economic system presumes a significant degree of virtue among its participants. As Michael Miller says, "When you lose a sense of trust and you have deep-seated greedy individuals separated from anything else, market economies fail. Market economies rely on an ethical structure. They didn't pop out of nowhere. They actually popped out of the Judeo-Christian tradition, especially in the Middle Ages, and they require certain kinds of people ... in order for them to sustain."

The Goodness of Work

Perhaps the most fundamental question when it comes to ethics in the marketplace has to do with work itself. Asking your neighbors or coworkers how they view their work can result in some very interesting responses. What gives their work its value? You could ask it this way: "If you won the lottery, would you continue to work? Why or why not?" Here are some of the reasons people give for why they work:

To avoid being on welfare
To pay for the weekends
To provide status and power
To enable them to retire comfortably
To support themselves and their families

Such reasons suggest that most people in the culture see their work primarily as a means to an end, even something to be avoided if possible. They see it as something they have to do until they can retire and do what they really want to do. Typically people see their work as a burden to be borne until they no longer have to work, and for many, the goal is to retire sooner rather than later. Interestingly, those are the same people who, in retirement, lament that they wish they had something meaningful to do with their lives!

It is true that part of the purpose for work is to provide for yourself and your dependents and to take care of yourself so that your extended family or the community doesn't have to. These are examples of what we call the "instrumental" value of work— work having value because of what else it accomplishes. Other examples of the instrumental value of work include being able to give to the poor; helping support charity, church, and nonprofit organizations; and being able to live out your faith publicly in the workplace.

But the goodness of work extends beyond its instrumental value. Work has intrinsic value as well. What this means is that the work itself that someone does has value beyond all of the other things it accomplishes. A Christian worldview provides rich resources for thinking about work in this way. God set it up so that work was an important component in paradise at the beginning of history and will be again at the end of history. For example, in the Bible's account of creation, the first human beings were mandated to work even though they were living in paradise, before the entrance of sin caused the world to be broken. The creation story links this to a basic human responsibility, that of exercising dominion over the world. Work was one of the primary ways in which human beings exercised this dominion.

British economist Sir Brian Griffiths suggests that this connection between work and dominion over the world is basic to economics. He says, "Human beings have been created with an urge to control and harness the resources of nature in the interests of the common good ... but are trustees to preserve and care for it. This process is precisely what an economist would refer to as 'responsible wealth creation.'"[1] And at the end of history, when the kingdom of God comes in its fullness, human beings will be working. When the Old Testament prophets envisioned the coming kingdom, they used metaphors that show work to be an important part of life. For example, the prophet Isaiah says, "They will beat their swords into plowshares and their spears into pruning hooks" (2:4). Implements of war will be transformed into implements of productive work. Thus, at the bookends of the Bible, work plays an important role. This suggests that work has value in and of itself, that it is an integral part of being human. Chuck Colson maintained, "We are indeed hardwired for work." It is part of our spiritual DNA. British writer Dorothy Sayers put it like this: "Work is the natural exercise and function of human beings — the creature who is made in the image of the Creator. Work is not primarily a thing that one does to live, but what one lives to do."[2]

To be sure, work is not always ideal, because it too has been tarnished by the brokenness of the world. That's why in the marketplace there are ethical tensions, scandals where the law is broken, employees exploited, customers defrauded, and even some ways of making money that are intrinsically evil, such as pornography. In addition, even in companies that treat their employees very well or in jobs where people feel like they have genuinely found their niche, there still may be days when employees want to quit. Work, though intrinsically good, has nonetheless been tainted by the brokenness of the world that is the result of the entrance of sin. But even seemingly degrading jobs can be a form of a person's service to God. When the New Testament addresses work, it often addresses slaves, who arguably did the most demeaning work available at that time. And slaves are told that their work is a component of their service to God — or to say it another way, their ministry (Col. 3:23 – 24).

Father Robert Sirico of the Acton Institute, a think tank on liberty and economics, provides a helpful summary of the moral dimension, which he refers to as stewardship, of the nobility of work. He says:

> I think that one of the reasons that work has such an incredible moral dimension is because there are very few other things that can touch so many aspects of human life whereby the work that we engage in, the property that we produce from that engagement, is so closely associated with ourselves, with our lives. It is a way in which we extend our life. If you consider it deeply enough, you'll understand that work exemplifies some of the most creative aspects of who human beings are. Human beings are not bound to things by instinct; animals are bound to things by instinct. Human beings are bound to things by the use of their reason, by their intellectual capacity, by their choices, and by a moral dimension that they bring to it. *So work is an extension and an expression of who human beings are*; this is why work has to be seen as possessing great dignity and it needs to be regarded very highly.

TOWARD A FLOURISHING ECONOMY

For work to resemble its original design requires a particular set of economic arrangements that also contribute to a properly functioning economy. Michael Miller explains, "A market economy, a free economy, requires a host of things. It requires private property, rule of law, so you need to have justice. It requires free association that people are allowed to get together to work together. It requires free exchange. But it also requires a culture of trust." Not every environment is fertile ground for a flourishing economy. We have learned over the centuries what conditions are necessary for economic life to prosper. Adam Smith, in his landmark work *The Wealth of Nations*, wrote these things down at the time our country was being established. He emphasized the importance of allowing people freedom to pursue their self-interest. And as a result of what he called "the invisible hand," the individual pursuit of self-interest results in the common good being advanced. Though he recognized the importance of moral values providing a means of restraint of self-interest, he also stressed how commerce civilizes human beings. Remember, for most of the history of civilization to that point, it was not uncommon for people and communities to resort to violence to secure the goods and services they needed. But Smith realized that to maximize your self-interest required civility, cooperation, service, and the providing of something of value for the community.

Michael Novak, in his important work *The Spirit of Democratic Capitalism*, uses the analogy of the three-legged stool to illustrate the conditions necessary for a flourishing economy.[3] He suggests that there are critical balancing factors necessary for a properly functioning economy. The economic system constitutes one leg of the stool, but he is clear that it cannot function alone. The market system is not self-correcting and needs the other two legs of the stool to stand. The most important of the other two legs is what he calls the "moral-cultural system," the system that essentially provides the moral checks and balances on the pursuit of self-interest by the participants in the economic system. This segment includes what he calls the "mediating structures," or the institutions that promote the moral values necessary for a healthy society. These stand in between the state and the individual and have the crucial function of preparing morally responsible citizens. They are voluntary organizations, such as schools, religious congregations, charitable groups, other volunteer groups — such as the YMCA, Boy Scouts, Girl Scouts, youth sports — and, of course, the most basic social institution, the family.

But these organizations can't provide all the necessary restraints on the economic system by themselves. There is also an important place for the political system and the law — Novak's third leg of the stool. The political system supplies critical infrastructure that is a big part of the fertile ground for a flourishing economy. It also functions as backstop if the moral-cultural system does not do its part in restraining self-interest. That is, the law steps in when the moral-cultural system fails, and given the expansion of laws and regulations governing more and more aspects of business and economic life, that's not an encouraging sign about the vitality of our moral-cultural system. To be sure, the law can't cover everything, and it is often an awkward tool for regulating aspects of the economy. Ethics is so important because it is able to touch on areas the law simply cannot — namely, one's motives and attitudes. In general, the law functions as the moral minimum, and it is not true that "if it's legal, it's moral."

Let's look more closely at what the political system/law provides that is necessary for a healthy economy. First, and maybe self-evident, is the *rule of law*. This is important because a good economy depends on a basic framework of law that provides for justice, prevents fraud, enforces contracts, and protects basic human rights. It is also important that the rule of law not be subject to corruption. It is not an accident that the countries that rank highest in the various corruption indices around the world often have the most stagnant economies and attract the least amount of foreign investment. The reason for this is that investors and entrepreneurs need assurances that business will be conducted based on the merits of the products and services being bought and sold, not on the ability to bribe the right officials. This is not to say that countries where there is corruption, such as India, cannot also have growing economies, but adherence to the rule of law is one of the important factors that make for fertile economic ground. Typically countries highest on the corruption index do not have many of the other important factors in place either.

A second important element the political system must provide for a healthy economy is *protection of private property*. Without this, there is no assurance that the hard work to get ahead and the risks to start a business will be rewarded. Private property provides the ultimate protection against the overreach of government, giving individuals a sphere that is off-limits to the hands of the state. The ability to accumulate property (not just real estate but wealth in general) is a critical incentive that gives hard work and risk taking the prospect of paying off. A good example of how this works involves the high tax rates on the wealthy around the world. In some countries in Europe, the tax rates for upper levels of income are around 75 percent, meaning that top earners don't get to keep much of what they make over a certain amount. They could be discouraged from taking additional risks to start businesses (which would result in the creation of new jobs) because they have to give so much of the income to the government. Thus, in many of these high-tax nations, the wealthy businesspeople choose to live in countries where the tax rates are lower, or they elect to avoid taking the additional risks of starting new businesses or growing existing ones.

Related to private property are other *incentives and protections for entrepreneurial activity*. The law must safeguard and encourage the initiative, innovation, and creativity that form the basis of new businesses and even new industries that produce the majority of new jobs in any economy. For example, patent laws are important because they protect the discoveries that make for new products and services. The law must also protect entrepreneurs and companies from having their products copied by firms that make knock-off products or that pirate software, music, and videos. The application and enforcement of patents for intellectual property is one of the most important protections the law can provide today, given that digital piracy is so common around the world.

Crucial to any healthy economy is the *availability of credit* and a secure banking system that channels savings and investment into capital for business. The credit freeze during the 2008 – 2009 financial crisis was so damaging to the economy because credit is the lifeblood of business. One key aspect to the availability of credit that the law can either encourage or hinder is the way property is "capitalized," that is, used as collateral for loans to start or grow businesses. Peruvian economist Hernando de Soto, in his important book *The Mystery of Capital*, argues that in many parts of the world, using one's property as collateral for a loan is either impossible or so time consuming and burdensome that it is discouraged.[4] In fact, in some countries that de Soto highlights, the documentation necessary to prove that you actually own your property (such as a title deed) is not readily available if available at all. The importance of credit is also the reason why capital gains and dividends are, and should be, taxed at lower rates than ordinary income. There needs to be sufficient incentive on the other side of the credit equation for those who take risks to invest their savings and thus provide the capital for business to function.

Other components of a healthy economy that the law must protect are basic rights, such as *the right to free association*, so that people can get together to work. A healthy economy requires cooperation at many levels that presume protection of this basic right. In addition, *a right to free exchange* is critical to a growing economy built on mutually beneficial exchanges. Essentially a market ought to be an association of individuals and organizations engaged in mutually beneficial exchanges.

As crucial as the legal framework is for a healthy economy, *a culture of trust and virtue* is just as key and something the law fundamentally cannot provide. Take the culture of trust. What makes that so important? Perhaps the best way to answer that is to tell you the story of one of my graduate students who came to the United States from Ethiopia to study. Tedla had major culture shock when he first arrived in the States. He told me that his dorm room at Biola University was the first place he had ever had a desk and chair of his own at which he could study. The first time he walked into the dining hall, he was so overwhelmed with the amount of food that he immediately walked out and vowed to skip one meal per day so as not to forget his roots. But the real shock to him was when, on his second day in the United States, I took him out for lunch. When it came time to pay the bill, I handed the server my credit card (Tedla had never seen a credit card before), and he processed the credit transaction, I signed the bill, and I indicated to Tedla that we could leave. He didn't know quite what to make of what had just occurred — I suspect he thought his ethics professor had just stolen our lunch! I explained a credit transaction to him — that the restaurant trusts that American Express will pay the charges and that American Express trusts I will pay the bill when it comes due in thirty days. He was quite surprised at the level of trust presumed for me to pay our bill. Even on our way out of the restaurant, he still had a nagging doubt that I had actually paid the bill! To say the least, he was not accustomed to that level of trust in commercial transactions where he was born and raised. To bring this point home to my students, I will often ask them, "How many of you would go out of your way to do business with people you trust?" Usually about half the hands go up, and not with a great level of conviction. But if I rephrase the question — "How many would go out of your way to avoid doing business with people you don't trust?" — all the hands go up very quickly, showing a much higher level of certainty.

Trust is a crucial virtue necessary for a healthy economy and a profitable business. Professor of international studies Francis Fukuyama, in his book *Trust*, suggests that culture is a critical determinant of whether a society is prosperous. He maintains specifically that an important part of the fertile ground for a growing economy is the degree of interpersonal trust among people who are not family members in a culture.[5] Especially in a global economy, with so many interconnected parts of the supply chain, the high degree of cooperation necessary for successful business means that trust enables business to be done with strangers outside of family ties. Fukuyama cites the prevalence of religious organizations as the market economy was being launched in the United Kingdom and the United States as a primary factor that built trust among non–blood relatives, so that business could be conducted with less oversight from government and lower costs to self-police the transactions and organizations. It is not hard to see how vital trust is for businesses that depend on repeat customers, which is the majority of businesses.

But it is also the case that lack of trust increases the cost of doing business within the organization, creating the need for costly oversight mechanisms and, in some cases, expensive compliance programs. Lack of trust in a company can also have intangible costs among employees, such as less willingness to "go the extra mile" for the company, less desire to embrace change, and generally less commitment to their work. Rather than greed being the engine that drives the economy, maybe we should say that trust is the lubricant that keeps the economic engine running smoothly. Perhaps instead of greed producing a vicious cycle in business, trust produces a virtuous cycle. With trust comes another important virtue, that of civility. This helps explain the puzzling statement of Adam Smith and his contemporaries that "commerce polishes and civilizes men." Remember, before the advent of the market system, it was not unusual for communities to resort to violence to get what they needed. With the market system, trade (mutually beneficial exchanges) became the main way people and communities obtained their necessary goods and services. Trust and civility became key virtues in this new way of doing business, because if a businessperson had neither of those virtues, people were less inclined to trade (do business) with him or her.

But it is not just trust and civility that market activity encourages. Other virtues are both required and nurtured by participation in the marketplace. These include the virtue of *service*. Try doing business without an emphasis on customer service. Legendary management professor Peter Drucker was well known for the maxim that "the purpose of business is to create a customer." Clearly, service was central to Drucker's idea of what a business is all about. In addition, the marketplace requires and nurtures *perseverance*, as the average salesperson who patiently cultivates and closes a sale over time can testify. This nurturing of perseverance is done particularly through adversity, as anyone who has been laid off or has had to lay off people can tell you. Also required and nurtured are *hard work, thrift, punctuality, promise keeping, creativity, innovation*, and *initiative*. Given how much of a person's waking hours are spent in the workplace, we shouldn't be surprised that the marketplace is also a crucible in which spiritual formation takes place, and a person's trust in God is nurtured there.[6] It is also true that the workplace is the occasion for a variety of vices, such as greed, dishonesty, fraud, and laziness. Opportunities for these vices to occur are the reason people face ethical dilemmas every day in their work.

CRITIQUE OF BUSINESS/CAPITALISM

Many people in the culture recognize that there are lots of occasions for vices to flourish in the marketplace and for business to do things that damage the common good of society. Corruption in the marketplace contributes to the general cultural cynicism about business alluded to earlier in this chapter. Often this critique extends to criticism of the market economy in general, and it is usually accompanied by a call for more government intervention in the marketplace. You see this criticism of business and capitalism in the films of Michael Moore, going as far back as the 1980s. In *Roger and Me*, Moore lampoons General Motors for closing an assembly plant in his hometown of Flint, Michigan, in the early 1980s. He continues his critique of corporate downsizing and outsourcing in the 1990s with *The Big One*. His most recent film, *Capitalism: A Love Story*, is a commentary on Wall Street in the aftermath of the financial crisis. Other films that focus on the financial crisis and the behavior of Wall Street banks include *Too Big to Fail*, *The Flaw*, *Margin Call*, and *Inside Job*.

Most of the criticisms of business center on some common themes. One is that business is fixated on greed, and by extension, the market system is based on greed. Moore, for example, charges that capitalism is a system of "legalized greed." Though there are numerous examples of companies that engage in illegal and unethical practices out of greed that can do very real harm to the community, we need to recognize that fundamentally greed is a matter of the heart, not the economic system. As Michael Miller says, "Greed is a human vice, not a capitalist vice." Adam Smith did not hold that "greed is good." That statement came from Ivan Boesky, a 1980s Wall Street trader who went to jail for insider trading. He made that statement, ironically, at one of the places most critical of business in the country, the University of California at

Berkeley. Smith distinguished between greed and self-interest, and he held that "enlightened self-interest" was central to the market economy. Remember that Smith was first and foremost a moral philosopher, not an economist, and his book *The Theory of Moral Sentiments* was written before *The Wealth of Nations*. The latter book is an application of his moral philosophy to the world of economics. He held that there are important moral values, such as justice and compassion, that should balance self-interest. That is not to say that these moral values always do what they are supposed to. Sometimes greed runs rampant and causes people to break the law, act unethically, and cause harm to the community. But to say that business is based on greed fails to make that important distinction between greed and self-interest.

A second common theme of criticism is that capitalism leads to a culture of consumerism and materialism that ultimately produces a profound spiritual poverty in individuals and communities. It is true that the market economy produces a level of wealth that previous generations could only dream of. But as with greed, materialism is essentially a part of the human condition, which emerges regardless of the economic system. It is also true that to maximize economic growth requires a consumerist culture. Though the drawbacks of the market system do include fostering materialism, the abundance of wealth produced by the market system provides unparalleled opportunities for charity and generosity. It is no accident that the United States is the most charitable nation on earth by far. Some of that has to do with the prevalence of religious groups that have charity as a central part of their teachings. But another big part of that is that the economy generates the affluence for substantial charity.

A third charge commonly leveled against business/capitalism is that the prosperity of the rich causes the poverty of the poor. That is, the wealth gained by the rich comes at the expense of the poor. You hear this echoed in the often repeated phrase "The rich get richer and the poor get poorer," implying that the rich getting richer is what is causing the poor to become poorer. This critique reflects what is known as a "zero sum game" view of economic life, that the size of the economic pie is relatively fixed, and if some get a larger piece, then others necessarily get a smaller one. If you imagine a family sitting around the dinner table while Mom cuts up the dessert pie, clearly if Dad gets the biggest piece, that leaves less for the others. What this means for economics in a zero sum view is that there is a necessary connection between the winners and losers, and the winners win at the expense of the losers.

To be clear, there are some places around the world where the zero sum view of economic life is pretty accurate. For example, many countries in the developing world of sub-Saharan Africa experience this. The wealthy get that way by theft, extortion, or abuse of political power — by extracting their wealth from others. Further, there are some aspects of the developed world where the zero sum view is more accurate, for example, in some of the trading desks on Wall Street or when the company's bonus pool for a given year is fixed. This view of economics also describes the ancient world in which the Bible was written, so that much of biblical caution about accumulation of wealth has to do with how it was accumulated, not its possession per se.

However, in modern industrial/information age economies, the zero sum view is not correct, and in many cases it reflects a misunderstanding of economics. In a growing, healthy economy, the size of the pie is constantly increasing as wealth is being created. In fact, every time someone makes a profit, wealth is created. If you start a company from nothing and in ten years it is worth $100 million, that wealth has been created by you and your employees' hard work, innovation, and initiative. Thus, in a market system it is possible to become wealthy without necessarily stealing from or taking advantage of others in the community. In other words, it is possible to do well financially *and* do good in terms of service to the community with your product/service at the same time. Of course, it is also possible to become wealthy by fraud, deception, and extortion, as the history of organized crime and recurring corporate scandals make clear. But the majority of people who are prosperous become that way by providing a useful product or service and thereby serving the community.

Though it is true that the market system is unparalleled at creating wealth, when it comes to distributing it, critics charge that is a different story. A fourth criticism of business/capitalism is that it causes growing inequality between rich and poor that some suggest is the great tragedy of our day. For example, theologian and adviser to President Barack Obama, Jim Wallis, insists that "the great crisis of American democracy is the division of wealth."[7] When viewed globally, the contrast between rich and poor is even sharper, and the inequalities are growing in the developed world as well. This is what economist Joseph Stiglitz calls "America's one percent problem."[8] The 1 percent at the top have a growing share of national income while the middle classes are being squeezed.

Though it is a cause for concern when people sense that social mobility is no longer available to them and that their inequality is set in stone, let's be clear about what the concern is. It can't be that inequality is inherently a problem, since we routinely accept all sorts of natural inequalities. For example, no matter how hard I work, I will never be an Olympic swimmer or NBA basketball player, because I don't have the physical tools to become either of those things. Some inequalities are the result of natural endowments, which we tend to accept as part of life. Further, it can't be that we believe in equality of outcome, that we would all end the race finishing at the same place, for we recognize the general principle that "you reap what you sow." Sometimes there are good reasons for inequalities. We uphold people who plan wisely, work hard, and save prudently. But we also recognize that some fall behind because of poor decisions about life's direction — dropping out of school, not applying themselves, or having children before being capable of supporting them. We should recognize a distinction between equality of outcome and equality of opportunity, the latter being very much worth fighting for.

The most egregious inequalities are the ones that are the result of injustice, which often makes inequalities worse. For example, it is unjust that someone is denied a job or a promotion because of racial or gender discrimination. It is unjust that inner-city children get substandard education in overcrowded and underfunded

schools that leaves them behind at the starting line, thus denying them equal opportunity. I am not saying that all inequalities
are the result of injustice, but some clearly are, and those are the
things that deserve society's moral passion and attention.

Historically, prior to the introduction of the market system,
there were staggering inequalities between the small handful of
royalty who owned virtually everything and the vast majority of
the population who lived in grinding poverty. Everywhere where
a market economy has been introduced, it has lifted the poor out
of poverty and created middle classes. Though critics are right
to point out extremes of wealth and poverty, those extremes are
substantially less in the free-market parts of the world. The vast
majority of the world's desperately poor are in sub-Saharan Africa,
where participation in the global economy has not occurred or the
conditions are not yet in place for the successful introduction of a
market economy. If the middle class is shrinking in a given society,
that is cause for concern. Or if the ability to better one's financial
condition is lost and people are stuck where they are, that is also
cause for concern. But inequality does not necessarily constitute
injustice — it may be unfortunate, but it is not necessarily unfair.

BUSINESS AND THE COMMON GOOD

We have seen that a healthy economy is built on the foundation
of a stable society in which the rule of law, private property, and
entrepreneurial activity are protected. Further, a healthy economy
both requires and nurtures many valuable virtues, such as trust
and hard work. But how does this translate to the level of individual companies and the businesspeople who run them? What is
the appropriate role for business to play in society? British writer
Charles Handy, writing in the *Harvard Business Review* in the
aftermath of the accounting scandals that brought down Enron,
WorldCom, and Arthur Andersen, asked the provocative question, "What's a business for?"[9] It may be very interesting for those
of you in business to ask that of your company: "What are we

in business for?" Or if you're not in business, think about asking that to your friends or neighbors who are. I suspect you would frequently get a look that said, *What a dumb question.* The most common answer would undoubtedly be, "To make money." Or they might put it in terms they learned in business school when asked, "What is the purpose of a corporation?" The answer would be something they likely memorized: "To increase the wealth of its shareholders."

Handy agrees that businesses have a duty to return a profit to the shareholders, or the technical owners of a public company. But he suggests it is an incomplete answer to the question "What's a business for?" He says:

> There is, first, a clear and important need to meet the expectations of a company's theoretical owners: the shareholders. It would, however, be more accurate to call most of them investors, perhaps even gamblers. They have none of the pride or responsibility of ownership and are, if truth be told, only there for the money.... But to turn shareholders' needs into a purpose is to be guilty of a logical confusion, to mistake a necessary condition for a sufficient one. We need to eat to live; food is a necessary condition of life. But if we lived mainly to eat, making food a sufficient, or sole purpose to life, we would become gross. *The purpose of a business, in other words, is not to make a profit, full stop. It is to make a profit so that the business can do something more or better.* That "something" becomes the real justification for the business. Owners know this. Investors needn't care.... Deep down, suspicions about capitalism are rooted in a feeling that its instruments, the corporations, are immoral in that they have no purpose other than themselves.[10]

Handy exemplifies the spirit of Adam Smith, who defended self-interest vigorously but also compared business to the professions, such as medicine and law. His point was that the bottom line was not really the bottom line for these professions. Rather, their goal was to serve the community, and if the service was provided with excellence, they could expect a reasonable standard of living. The income they derived from their service was an expected by-product, not the goal. It was conceived as a moral role in society, to serve the common good. The idea that a business exists solely to make money is a more recent view, different from the traditional role that business had a moral role to fulfill in society.

Dallas Willard points out the irony in the way business presents itself to the community, noting that it is often very different from the self-perception of companies and their executives.

> No business or other profession advertising its "services" announces to the public that it is there for the purpose of enriching itself or those involved in it. All will say with one accord that their purpose is service. I have never met any professionals who would tell their clients that they were there just for their own self-interest. Still, many professionals today are dominated by self-interest, and that is the source of the constant stream of moral failures that occupies our courts and [the news].[11]

Willard cites John Ruskin, writing in 1860, as an example of the way business was portrayed that is much closer to the spirit of Adam Smith than to today's business culture. Ruskin states about the businessperson, "It is no more his function to get profit for himself out of [providing for the community] than it is a clergyman's function to get his stipend. The stipend is a due and necessary adjunct, but not the object of his life, if he be a true clergyman, any more than his fee (or *honorarium*) is the object of life to a true physician. Neither is his fee the object of life to a true merchant. All three, if true men, have a work to be done."[12] That work is what constitutes their purpose.

I'm not saying that profit is a bad thing. I would suggest quite the contrary. Of course, profit is necessary for a business to continue to exist. Profit is also a very important market signal that a business is deploying its resources efficiently. If a company is losing money, that is a signal that something is wrong and needs to be fixed. Conversely, increases in profit indicate resources are being used more efficiently now than in the past. We should acknowledge that profit is an indicator of efficiency, not necessarily anything more. Just because a company is highly profitable does not mean it is engaged in good business — that is, business that provides a good service to the community. If profit measured that, then pornography and illegal drugs would constitute some of the best businesses around. So profit necessarily measures the efficiency of the means, not necessarily the worthiness of the ends being pursued by the business.

So let's be clear — what is a business for? It has two primary purposes — to serve the common good of the community with goods and services that contribute to human flourishing and to provide meaningful work that develops its employees. As with the professions, if those things are done with excellence, the owners/ shareholders can expect a reasonable, or fair, rate of return on their investment. Let's think about the good that business does simply by virtue of doing its job well. Handy summarizes:

> By creating new products, spreading technology, and raising productivity, business has always been the active agent of progress. It helps make the good things of life affordable to ever more people. This process is driven by competition and spurred on by the need to provide adequate returns to those who risk their money and their careers, *but it is, in itself, a noble cause.*... The pursuit of a cause does not have to be the prerogative of charities and the not-for-profit sector. Nor does a mission to improve the world make business into a social agency.[13]

It is not uncommon to see business in its service role when it is doing something charitable. But Handy's point, and the one I am making here, is that business serves the community simply by virtue of doing its business. Business serves the community primarily by the products and services it makes available in response to the demands and needs of its customers. Further, it serves by employing people from the community and providing them with both meaningful work and a means of supporting themselves and their dependents. By making a profit, business also serves its investors, many of whom are pension funds, 401(k) funds, and college funds, with people who are dependent on their investments for retirement and college. Business also serves the community by paying its taxes and contributing to the tax base (thereby making public services available) and complying with the various laws and regulations. Though it seems that the most visible service of business is when it is involved in charity, we should not minimize the good that business does simply by virtue of being in business. This is why as a culture we should not be so quick to demand that business "give back" to the community, since this demand presumes that companies are in the business of extracting from the community and thus need to give something back to balance the scales. I'm not saying that there aren't some companies who are indeed guilty of extracting value from the public. But to characterize business in general that way is misleading and overlooks the way business actually benefits the public interest.

But recognizing the good that business does also means that business has the potential to do harm to the communities they are designed to serve. Of course, business does harm when it violates the law, as is the case when companies engage in fraud or violate environmental laws. But even legal business can do damage to the public interest. Bob Rowling, president of Omni Hotels, made a difficult decision about a part of the business he believed was doing harm. He describes the situation:

> We got into the hotel business in the early '90s and acquired Omni (hotel chain) in 1996. In about 1999, we made the decision to remove pornography from our hotels. I've been asked why we made that decision. A lot of things went into it. For one thing, when we first got into business in the early '90s, hotels showed R-rated movies, and we saw a progression over a five- or six-year period, where the content became more and more XXX-rated. So in the late '90s, we decided that we were going to pull the pornography out of

all our hotels. The decision was not without some internal debate in our company. We had people who maintained that it could cost us a lot of revenue. About 60 percent of the movie revenue that comes into hotels is from pornography. There has never been a debate in our society, I think, that pornography denigrates women. It destroys families, and it leads to crime. There is no redeeming societal benefit to pornography, and in fact just the opposite, it actually ruins people's lives. People become addicted to it. It was an interesting response when we pulled it.... Over the years we have had over one hundred thousand emails, letters, and thank-yous. Letters from men who say, "Look, I travel on business. I have a wife and a family. I'm tempted when I go to a hotel that offers pornography. Thank you for pulling it out." We made a decision that we thought was going to cost us money. I think, because of the good public relations that came with it ... we have actually at least broken even. I don't think it's cost us a dime, by being a good corporate responsible citizen.

HELP FOR THE BUSINESSPERSON

Business can do harm as well as do good. The late philosopher Irving Kristol remarked that we should give two cheers, not three, to business — not three, because of its potential to do harm. This raises a very important question that Princeton professor David Miller summarizes like this: "What makes one company tilt from starting out as ethical and moral and decent to suddenly failing and finding themselves doing the 'perp walk' someday?" That is, what factors help an organization establish and maintain an environment conducive to ethical behavior, to doing good rather than doing harm?

It is critical to recognize that the culture of the organization matters a great deal and that leaders are the culture carriers of the company. Former General Electric CEO Jack Welch described the importance of the corporate culture:

It happens to be one of the most immutable rules of business. *Soft culture matters as much as hard numbers.* And if your company's culture is to mean anything, you have to hang—publicly—those in your midst who would destroy it. It is a grim image, we know. But the fact is, creating a healthy, high-integrity organizational culture is not puppies and rainbows. And yet, for some reason, too many leaders think a company's values can be relegated to a five-minute conversation between HR and a new employee. Or they think culture is about picking which words—do we "honor" our customers or "respect" them?—to engrave on a plaque in the lobby. What nonsense. An organization's culture is not about words at all. It is about behavior—and consequences. It is about every single individual who manages people knowing that his or her key role is that of *chief values officer*, with enforcement powers to match. It is about knowing that at every performance review, employees are evaluated for both their numbers *and* their values.[14]

Welch was highlighting the difference between ethics and compliance. Compliance has to do with regulations and the law—standards imposed by those outside the organization, usually lawyers or regulatory bodies. Ethics, by contrast, has to do with the defining values of the organization that animate its mission and give tangible direction to its decisions. Ethics comes from within the organization and must be "owned" by employees who have to see it modeled from the top.

Leaders must be aware of the various pressures employees face that can undermine the ethical culture of the organization. Consider, for example, the pressure to "get along by going along." This can be very strong in a company, as most organizations work very hard to socialize employees into their way of doing things. This philosophy provides an important sense of group cohesion and teamwork but can also inhibit employees from challenging the consensus of the group. When taken to an extreme, it can create an environment where groupthink occurs and people who question the consensus end up being marginalized in the organization if not outright fired. In addition, leaders should be cognizant that most people, including adults, are followers when it comes to ethics and need to be empowered to voice their convictions even if they go against the grain in the organization.

Business leaders cannot assume the employees they hire will all have properly functioning moral compasses. Given the fracturing of the family that has occurred in the past twenty to thirty years, it is naive to think this generation of potential employees has not been affected. Growing up in the culture of relativism described in chapters 1 and 2 hasn't helped produce a stable set of moral values to which they adhere. As a result, when people join a company's workforce, they are not finished products and may need further training in ethics from the organization. I'm not saying that companies are in the ethics business, but they cannot ignore this dimension when it comes to employee growth and development. This means that not only must the expectations be clear and modeled by those to whom employees report, but the organizations must also enforce those expectations with a "carrot and stick" approach. That means incentives for upholding those values and, as Sherron Watkins, the Enron whistle-blower, suggests, "a zero tolerance policy for the ethically challenged."[15]

Sometimes it is employers' unrealistic expectations of employees that provide the pressure to act unethically. For example, in the late 1990s, Sears Auto Centers across California were caught and fined heavily for selling unneeded repair work systematically over a period of years. Not only were the service advisers paid on commission, but they reported being given unreasonably high sales quotas, and if they didn't hit them, their jobs were in jeopardy. They felt that to keep their jobs, they had no choice but to sell parts and services that were not needed. Leaders need to be aware that though they need to push and challenge their employees to be their best, when expectations are not workable, people will bend the rules in order to meet them, especially if their jobs or wages are on the line.

There is more to the corporate culture than making sure the

values and standards are clear, reasonable, and modeled at the top of the organization. Employees need to have a sense of purpose in their work, that what they are doing is significant and is making a difference. David Miller says:

> For a lot of it, it's the people in the organization. Do they have a sense of vision and meaning and purpose for what they're doing? If they think they're just making chairs or glasses or pens, something simple, a functional widget, they don't really care. But if they see ... that what they do some-how makes society a better place, somehow provides goods and services, they ignite, they come alive, and they will be proud of their company. They will also stand up for it.

Bill Pollard, former CEO of ServiceMaster, concurs: "People want to contribute to a cause, not just earn a living."[16] He cites the example of one of his employees in the janitorial service division of the company who had been cleaning hospital floors for many years.

> Why is Shirley Nelson, a housekeeper in a 250-bed commu-nity hospital, still excited about her work after 15 years? She certainly has seen some changes. She actually cleans more rooms today than she did five years ago. The chemicals, the mop, and the housekeeping cart have all been improved. Nevertheless, the bathrooms and the toilets are the same. The dirt has not changed nor have the unexpected spills of the patients or the arrogance of some of the physicians. So what motivates Shirley? Shirley sees her job as extending to the welfare of the patient and as an integral part of a team that helps sick people get well. She has a cause that involves the health and welfare of others. When Shirley first started, no doubt she was merely looking for just a job. But she brought to her work an unlocked potential and a desire to accomplish something significant. As I talked with Shirley about her job, she said, "If we don't clean with a quality effort, we can't keep the doctors and nurses in business.

We can't serve the patients. *This place would be closed if we didn't have housekeeping.*" Shirley was confirming the reality of our mission. She was in command of her work, of herself, and of her own small piece of our business. And in a very real sense she was leading me, by talking about her work, her customers, and her role in our shared mission.[17]

Pollard is highlighting a crucial part of the company's culture — that employees see themselves as part of something bigger than themselves and their paychecks that gives them pride in their work and their organization and makes them culture carriers in the day-to-day work of the company.

Even in corporate cultures that function the way Pollard and Welch describe, there are still ethical challenges to be faced, where the right thing is clear but difficult and costly to do. There are also ethical dilemmas to be confronted, where it is not always clear what the right thing is. First, let's be clear about the connection between ethics and the law. The law is the moral minimum, the moral floor, not the ceiling. If someone insists, "If it's legal, it's moral," that's a red flag that indicates a dangerous rationalization is occurring. The famous Soviet dissident Aleksandr Solzhenitsyn described what happens culturally when the law replaces ethics: "A society with no other scale but the legal one is not quite worthy of man. . . . The letter of the law is too cold and formal an atmosphere of moral mediocrity, paralyzing man's noblest impulses."[18] Compliance and ethics are not the same thing, though there may be some overlap, so we must be careful not to mistake a company's compliance program for ethics.

Let's also be clear about the link between good ethics and good business, between ethical behavior and profitability. From a Christian worldview, by definition good ethics is always good business, since good business encompasses more than the bottom line. But what most people mean when they ask if good ethics is good business is whether good ethics makes a company more profitable. In the short run, good ethics is almost always costly. Robert George summarized it like this: "In the short run, it can cost you money.

It might even put your business in jeopardy, so it takes ... a strong moral sense and a strong will to be able to take those risks." If good ethics were always good business, then everyone would do good business all the time. There would be no need for discussion of business ethics, and this chapter would be unnecessary!

In the long run, a better case can be made for connecting ethics and profitability due to the trust that good ethics fosters both with customers and within the organization. But there are still exceptions to this, with companies who are so strong in their industries that they can act unethically with customers, and it is not realistic to think the market will punish them for it. But in general, in the long run, a good case can be made for the connection between good ethics and good business. For example, in the aftermath of the Enron debacle, *Business Week* had this on their cover: "25 Ideas for a Changing World." At the top of the list was an item directly related to ethics: "Executives are learning that trust, integrity and fairness do matter — and are crucial to the bottom line."[19]

Of course, whether good ethics is profitable or not is not the central issue. We want people to do the right thing in the marketplace because it's right, not just because it's advantageous. This was the point of the provocative *Harvard Business Review* article "Why Be Honest If Honesty Doesn't Pay?" The authors argued that "business men and women keep their work because they want to, not because it pays."[20] I would quibble with their premise that honesty doesn't pay, as I have argued earlier, but they are certainly right that fundamentally we want people to be ethical in the workplace because it's right. Though if it does pay, that's an added bonus that provides an additional incentive for people to do the right thing.

One common strategy for dealing with the ethical challenges in the marketplace is to compartmentalize one's life — to have one set of moral rules for the workplace and a different set for private life. Ray Kroc, founder of McDonald's, appears to have taken this view and was reported to have said, "My priorities are God first, family second, and McDonald's hamburgers third. But when I go to work on Monday morning, that order reverses."[21] Though it is hard to be certain about what Kroc was thinking when he said this, he is commonly understood to mean that to succeed in the marketplace requires two different sets of priorities, one for work and one for private life, and two corresponding sets of moral rules. Though this may be a common perception about what it takes to compete in the marketplace, this kind of dichotomy about life and the dissonance it creates is hard to maintain in the long run. Further, from a Christian worldview, all of life is to come under the lordship of Christ. The idea of compartmentalizing such a significant area of life as your work is contrary to the common biblical understanding of life being a unified whole.

It is true that the application of some important moral values and virtues might look different in different arenas because the relationships are different. For example, in my role as a professor, the moral value of compassion will likely be applied somewhat differently with my students than it would with my twentysomething and teenage boys. But that doesn't mean there are two different sets of values/rules for those different spheres of influence. This dual morality that results from compartmentalization is very problematic and is not the solution to handling ethical challenges and dilemmas.

Sometimes you are in the position where you are pressured to do something clearly illegal or unethical. If you are asked to do something illegal, graciously but firmly refuse and cite the legal risk you would be taking to do such a thing. Sometimes people are unaware of the liability to which they are exposing themselves, even when doing things that may not be technically illegal but are clearly unethical. For example, one of my graduate business students was the trainer for a software sales staff who was training the sales force on a new product they were releasing. He knew the product was not ready for sale, but he was ordered to train the sales staff to sell it as though it were free of all the bugs they knew were in it. They were committed to supporting the product and would fix all the problems, but they were especially anxious to get it to market sooner rather than later. My teaching colleague, who is an attorney, informed him of the legal liability to which he was exposed by essentially training sales staff to perpetrate a sales fraud. He really got the trainer's attention when he told him that he would have little basis on which to defend him if he were called on it.

Not everything is black and white, however. In fact, there is a considerable amount of gray in many ethical challenges. It may be that there are some things more personal than ethical. For example, my friend Jim runs a medium-sized advertising agency in our community, and for years he has refused to take on any accounts of tobacco companies. He readily admits that this is a deeply personal thing for him — his dad smoked all his life and died of a heart attack at age fifty. Although Jim is not thrilled about supporting tobacco in any way, he acknowledges that it is a legal product that has the right to advertise, and he doesn't think another company is doing anything necessarily unethical by taking its business. In more personal matters, companies are often sensitive to these things, and if you have been a good employee and are valued by the company, they will often try their best to accommodate you if you approach them graciously.

But sometimes there is a moral component to what makes you uncomfortable with an assignment from your bosses. Take the example of Sarah. Upon graduation from college, Sarah takes a position at a small firm (twenty employees) that specializes in web design and management services for business clients. After nine months on the job, she is given the opportunity to take the lead role on a project for a new client that everyone around the firm has referred to as "the big kahuna." The company is a leading apparel manufacturer and retailer that has sought to create an edgy and somewhat rebellious image. One marketing campaign, which used posters in dormitories and full-page ads in college newspapers, featured drinking games and party drink mixes, prompting some activists to accuse the company of encouraging underage drinking. At an initial project conceptual design meeting, Sarah meets marketing executives from the client company who express their desire for a website that "attracts a lot of traffic by capitalizing on the brand identity and image we have worked so hard to successfully create." After the meeting, Sarah meets with a senior executive of her firm named Lynn. Sarah shares with Lynn that this assignment is especially troubling to her because her cousin was killed in a car accident a few years ago in which underage drinking played a part. Lynn suggests she take the assignment because of the influence she can have on it.

For Sarah, this assignment is personal, but it also has a moral component — the portrayal of underage drinking. The company insists that all the actors used in the scenes are of age, though they may look young. This is an example of a gray area that mixes the personal and moral. Think about what will happen if Sarah turns down the assignment, or if she has no choice and instead quits her job. Chances are very good that the person who replaces her will have less of a conscience than she does. There is a case to be made for "keeping her place at the table" and attempting to use her influence on this project and on others in the future, unless there are compelling reasons to walk away. One of the ways to exert her influence is to appeal to the company's brand image in the marketplace and ask if these are the kinds of projects for which they wish to be known. For example, my friend Jim, who has the advertising agency, won't take ad campaigns that feature heavy use of sex because that's not what he wants his agency to stand for. In addition, he knows he would lose other lucrative clients if his agency became known for the use of sexual persuasion.

Even if it is clear to you what the right thing is, you must approach it strategically in order to facilitate change. Just because you are dealing with a moral matter, don't think you can ride in on the moral high ground, make a grand pronouncement, and effect a change. Moral issues require the same kind of strategic thinking in order to make a change in the organization. Harvard Business School ethics professor Joseph Badaracco insists, "The vast majority of difficult, important human problems [I would add, ethical ones too] — both inside and outside organizations are not solved by a swift, decisive stroke from someone at the top. What usually matters are careful, thoughtful, small, practical efforts by people working far from the limelight."[22] Sometimes you have to dig deeper to gather and clarify all the facts, and you have to be sure you have sufficient organizational capital banked to take on the issue about which you're concerned. Sometimes it means crafting compromises that leave you ultimately unsatisfied, but that is as much as you can accomplish. Though it may sound odd, at times you have to settle for limited objectives on some things that have moral overtones, unless you determine, unwisely in my view, that everything that has moral implications is a "hill worth dying on."

And sometimes you do have to walk away from an assignment, or even from a job, because of your moral reservations. But how do you know when you've reached that point? Drawing a hard and fast line is tricky in these cases, but here are some criteria that will help you make that decision. First, does what you are being asked to do put you in *legal jeopardy*? No job is worth the risk of going to jail or being sued. If you need to consult with an attorney either formally or informally to clarify this, do so. Then come back to the company and give them the legal opinion you've received.

Second, does the activity in question constitute something that is *intrinsically evil* with which you cannot participate? For example, one of my business students who graduated and went into the real estate business was asked to work on a deal to lease space for the business operation of the largest and best-known producers of pornography in the world. My teaching colleague and I advised him to walk away from that. Or take my friend who was doing information systems consulting and was asked to work on an arrangement that would enable the phone company to more effectively bill and collect from its 976 (dial-a-porn) customers. He was eventually told he would not be on the project but would have asked for another assignment had he been asked.

A third criterion comes out of a distinctly Christian worldview. Would your coworkers experience *cognitive dissonance* (a "What's wrong with this picture?" moment) if they found out that you, a Christian, were working on questionable assignments? Would what you work on undermine you ability to live out your faith on the job?

A fourth, and more subjective, criterion is this — is what you are being asked to do, over time, *corrosive to your soul*? Does it chip away at the core of who you are?

These criteria may not always be determinative, but they do raise points of concern and tension. In other words, they may not always be "red lights" indicating a stop but "yellow lights" indicating the need to slow down and proceed cautiously.

CONCLUSION

In this chapter, I have attempted to highlight the good that business does and the opportunities we have to honor God with our work. Business both requires and fosters some very important virtues, such as trust, service, perseverance, initiative, and creativity — what might be called "entrepreneurial traits." Of course, the marketplace also presents many opportunities to act unethically, and business can do harm as well as good. Former Baylor University business professor Donald Schmeltekopf summarizes the good that business does:

> It is important to remember the ways that business has contributed to our individual and collective life in America and around the world. American businesses employ approximately 55 percent of all United States citizens in the workforce. Indeed, business activity constitutes the backbone of an economy that makes possible the high standard of living we enjoy in this country. Business has been responsible for the enhanced technology that has largely replaced the drudgery of most manual labor, a consequence in part of the inventiveness of business and its willingness to take and bear the burden of financial risk. No institution is more responsive to the demands of its constituents than business. We must note as well that businesses pay a large share of the taxes that help to support our common defense, ensure safety in our homes and cities, and provide the necessary social services from which we all benefit. And

there can be little doubt that most business firms conduct their affairs as good citizens of our various communities.[23]

This view of business as doing good for the community generates a responsibility to the community to ensure that good, not harm, is indeed being done. This is why ethics is so important and why the law alone cannot provide the framework for a market economy to flourish. For to be free and prosperous, we need also to be virtuous.

CHAPTER 6

Ethics in
Public Life

Can government be an instrument of good and of justice and promote human flourishing? Chuck Colson described a time when government was a powerful agent for good in the world. This was in 1972, just before Colson left the White House on an assignment as special counsel to President Richard Nixon, to go to the Soviet Union to negotiate a very important agreement to limit the USSR's development of nuclear weapons in exchange for the United States providing them with badly needed grain. The agreement was moving along through Congress, and as Colson was about to embark for the USSR, members of Congress added an amendment to the agreement that would allow Jews who wanted to emigrate from the USSR to Israel to leave freely, something they had been prohibited from doing up to that point. Colson described his discussions with the chief Soviet negotiator, Vasili Kuznetsov, as they went back and forth about the issue of the USSR allowing the Jews to leave.

> We sat at one of those long tables, with all of the Americans on one side and all of the Soviets on the other side,

and went for about two hours. This guy [Kuznetsov] was really tough, and he kept saying to me, "Mr. Colson, you come here, and you are trying to interfere with our domestic affairs." And I kept countering him, saying, "No, human rights aren't domestic affairs. You don't give human rights to people in the government, and you can't take them away. *Human rights are God-given.*" I remember quoting the language of the Declaration of Independence, and he's getting angrier and angrier and angrier. And I learned, ahead of time, that what to do with him is you keep pressing him. And so I just kept getting tougher and tougher. I said, "We're not interfering in your domestic affairs. *We're talking about human rights.*" And after about two hours, you could see everybody was getting tense, and he was beginning to weaken. And all of sudden, he hit the table and said, "Okay, Mr. Colson, you can tell your president we'll do our part." As a result of that, within days thereafter, they released 35,000 Soviet Jews. But what I learned out of that was that the unique contribution that America makes to the world, and it is unique, is to promote the idea that people are created equal and endowed by their Creator with certain inalienable rights. This is the fundamental ethic on which the Western civilization was built.

Robert George insists this protection of fundamental human rights is one of the most important roles of government, and leadership is acting unethically if they are not doing this well. George maintains that, "quoting our Founding Fathers, 'We hold these truths to be self evident: that all men are created equal, that they're endowed by their Creator with certain inalienable rights. And among these are life, liberty, and the pursuit of happiness.' And then it goes on to say that it is fundamentally for the protection of these rights that governments are instituted among men." Historian Glenn Sunshine expands on this by arguing that government doesn't either give or take away these fundamental rights. He says, "One thing that I think is particularly important in current political discussions is to highlight the fact that rights don't come from government. Rights, our inalienable rights, are endowed by our Creator. It is something that's inherent to what it means to be human. And government exists to protect those rights. It doesn't grant those rights. It recognizes them."

Let's be more specific about the role of government, because whether government is capable of doing good partially depends on the prior question of its proper role in society. Chuck Colson summarized the role of government: "Its job is to preserve order, to do justice, *and to promote human flourishing*. In the biblical understanding, that's what a government does." Michael Miller, citing President James Madison, adds, " 'The first task of government is to create order and secure rights and liberty. *And then, the second task is to restrain the governors.*' And so, this is where you need government, but you need a limited government. And the root of this, of course, is what Christians understand as the doctrine of original sin. You have to limit power because of its tendency to corrupt."

THE ROLE OF GOVERNMENT

Our views of the proper role of government developed historically over time out of roots from two of the greatest thinkers of the medieval period, Augustine and Thomas Aquinas. Each had somewhat different views of human nature and, thus, of the roles of government. Augustine had a very pessimistic view of human nature, comparing government's role to constructing a "peace among robbers." He held to two different realms of social life, which he called "the city of God" and "the city of man." The city of God is the realm of redemption and the church, and the city of man is the realm of preservation and human government. Augustine's social vision was highly individualistic, with society composed of individuals seeking to maximize their self-interest. Social reality was viewed by Augustine through the lens of conflicting pursuits of self-interest. It is fundamentally a conflict model of society. Thus the social world is disordered, full of lustful self-interest. Sin has corrupted the cosmos, and God has sovereignly saved some out of this corruption by grace. God has permitted the establishment of government to maintain minimal peace and harmony. However, the ability of people in society to create government indicates that society does not entirely revolve around conflict. There is some ability toward cooperation that is part of the image of God in human beings. Therefore his social ethic is not so much about social progress but about a balance of power and the achievement of a rough justice. In other words, we are to do the best we can here, knowing that perfect justice is only found in eternal life. Augustine had a great influence on later theologians, such as Martin Luther and Reinhold Niebuhr and the political philosopher Thomas Hobbes.

Theologian Thomas Aquinas put a somewhat different social vision forth a few centuries later. Aquinas marked a return to the strong connection between ethics and politics that characterized the ancient Greek thinkers, such as Plato and Aristotle. He saw human beings as essentially social beings, and he reasoned that even if human beings were not morally broken due to the entrance of sin, there would still be a place for government and the state. He saw society through the lens of harmony, not conflict. Aquinas's social vision was a vision of order and harmony. He saw human society as an organism, in which each part ideally related in harmony. He emphasized the world being God's good creation and one of those good things being the innate inclination of humans to live in society. The way in which human beings get together in social relations reflects the goodness in creation and is not some sort of arrangement to ensure one's survival, as Augustine suggested. Thus social life is founded on human nature being in the image of God, not human nature as corrupted by sin. Social life together is necessary for the development of a person's potentialities. For Aquinas, institutions exist to encourage the development of good people, a philosophy that reflects the ancient Greek emphasis on developing public virtue. But for Augustine, by contrast, institutions, namely government, exist to restrain fundamentally bad people. To put it very simply, the Augustinian vision for government was limited and restricted to restraining essentially evil human beings. For Aquinas, however, government exists to enable human flourishing more broadly, promoting what the ancient Greeks called "public virtue."

Augustine and Aquinas were followed by the "big three" of political philosophy during the Enlightenment period, Thomas Hobbes, John Locke, and Jean-Jacques Rousseau. These three are widely considered to be the seminal thinkers who provided the philosophical framework for Western democracy. Hobbes was a realist in terms of his political philosophy, following the social vision of Augustine. Society is the place where free and equal individuals clash to maximize self-interest. The goal of government is to provide minimal order to safeguard one's pursuit of self-interest. Hobbes viewed society as a voluntary association, not a divine order in which all have their ordained place with little social mobility. In addition, he stressed the relationship of the ruler with the will of the people, opening the door for the later development of the idea of the consent of the governed. Though he also left the door open to totalitarianism, this is tied to his view of the state of nature — the war of all against all. Hobbes was concerned that with freedom and individual rights, there was also the likely prospect of anarchy, which led him to suggest a totalitarian solution in a powerful ruler he figuratively called "Leviathan."

John Locke had perhaps the greatest influence on American democracy. He had extensive exposure to European Calvinists, being raised in Scotland and having lived for a time with the French Calvinists (Huguenots). His social ethic was also driven by realism, but his was aimed specifically at government, not at society as a whole. His concern was with totalitarianism and limiting the will and power of government. He had the same acquisitive view of human nature as Hobbes, but his was rooted in nature due to sin. He was concerned about the self-interest of the rulers more than the individuals in the society, and his system placed limits on the rulers.

For Locke, natural rights were ultimately theologically grounded. Since rights are natural, from creation, people must consent to be governed. The state is limited by his notion of the right to property. Property, according to Locke, was the best guarantor of liberty because it marked out a sphere into which the state could not intervene. Property was grounded theologically, in the creation mandate, with man seen as co-creator with God, unlocking the creation. It was also grounded in his view of human nature. He continued Hobbes's view of a human being as an acquisitive individual and added to it the view that people have a right over their own bodies. Thus the labor of people's bodies can produce goods to which they are entitled as fruit of their labor. The acquisitive nature of humankind is satisfied by the accumulation of property, which also keeps the state from overreaching its bounds. However, the right to property was not absolute, since a person was only entitled to what he or she could reasonably use. This was a reaction to the enormous feudal estates that hoarded goods at the expense of the rest of the population.

Rousseau, like Hobbes, was concerned about rampant individualism. He saw a different source for humankind's evil, namely, that people were inherently good and had been corrupted by institutions (particularly those of competitive capitalism with their resulting inequalities). His philosophy of the state of nature was similar to that of Hobbes, and he held that humankind was driven out of the state of nature and into civil society by the need for self-preservation (which he referred to as the social contract). However, he held a more positive role for society than simply keeping the peace. Since institutions could corrupt people, they could also lift people up and improve them. He held that both the inclinations toward good and evil are found in presocial humans (in the state of nature) but that society has developed the tendencies toward evil more than the tendencies toward good. He was concerned about the absolutist claims of the monarch and the tyranny of individuals that resulted from the accumulation of wealth and power. But he feared even more the corrosive effects of rampant individualism, especially that which was empowered by wealth and power. As with Hobbes, he tended toward totalitarianism, and the founders of the American republic adopted his diagnosis but not his cure. They essentially adopted Locke's cure instead.

The contributions of these three men to modern political philosophy were immense. They transformed the view of the society to a voluntary association, which laid the framework for a more fully developed idea of government by consent of the governed. The draconian and totalitarian solutions of Hobbes and Rousseau to the problem of rampant individualism were not adopted by the American Founding Fathers due to the strong moral consensus provided by Christian faith that kept the corrosive effects of individualism in check. To be sure, there was a need for government to ensure that fundamental rights and the common good were protected. But given Locke's Puritan/Calvinistic roots, it is not surprising that he emphasized limits on the rulers rather than limits on the individuals in society.[1]

The American founders assumed that a healthy, functioning civil society in which freedom was protected required virtue among the citizenry. In fact, the notion of freedom was actually quite different than how it is understood today. The founders stressed that freedom involved the individual liberty to follow one's conscience, to do what a person thought was right. That is quite different from the individualism of today, which views freedom as the liberty to do whatever one chooses, acting out of desire and preference, not necessarily on principle. The founders did not separate government and morality, nor did they separate religion from the morality that informs government. In fact, they held that freedom required virtue to keep it from becoming corrosive to the culture — and that morality required the nourishment of religion to keep it vibrant. For example, in his farewell address after his second term as president, George Washington said, "Religion and morality are indispensable supports to political prosperity.... Reason and experience both forbid us to expect that national morality can prevail in exclusion of religious principle." James Madison echoed this belief in the Northwest Ordinance, the official government charter for settling the Northwest Territories. "Religion, morality, and knowledge, being necessary to good government and the happiness of mankind, shall be forever encouraged."[2] The founders thus drew from the Augustinian model of society, with its pessimism about human nature, including that of the governors, and the need to protect individuals from government. In addition, they took the notion that the role of government was a limited one and focused on protecting rights and procuring order and justice. But they also drew from the tradition of Aquinas (called the "Thomistic tradition") that government had a role in promoting virtue among the citizens. The founders recognized that much of that came from other social institutions, such as the family, schools, and religious/voluntary associations, but that the state also had a role in fostering the virtue necessary for freedom to flourish.

LAW AND MORALITY

We must be clear about the connection between law and morality. A more recent tradition known as "legal positivism" is the view that valid law is whatever the lawmakers decide, and whatever social customs and standards are recognized by the officials are authoritative. Whether the law is effective, just, or prudent is not related to whether the law in question is valid or not. This tradition stands in sharp contrast to an earlier and long-standing natural-law legal tradition that insists that valid laws are grounded in the moral law, which I argued in chapter 2 does exist and can be known. The rise of legal positivism coincided with the erosion of belief in natural law and the general movement toward relativism that I have already described. That is, skepticism about the existence of moral law that can be the basis for civil law is what generated the alternative of legal positivism.

I have already said there is a moral law that can be known and is the basis for pursuing virtue and making our laws. But a common refrain in the culture today is "You can't legislate morality." Michael Miller responds, however, "Of course you can; that's what law is: it is the legislation of morality. It is rooted in a moral order, and if the government violates those rights, then it is wrong and it should be changed." He is pointing out that government as well is under the moral law, and that it is not only possible, but also not surprising, that government can violate it. Our Founding Fathers recognized that prospect and empowered the people to change their government if it tried to legislate morality.

Let's be clear about exactly what we can legislate. When people claim that morality can't be legislated, they generally mean that a moral *intention* cannot be the subject of the law. On that point, they are certainly right to claim that a person's motives cannot be established by the law. But if we mean by morality moral *behavior*, then they're wrong, since all law is the legislation of someone's morality. Most every law has some moral component to it. Take, for example, something that appears morally neutral, such as traffic laws. They are hardly without a moral dimension, since almost all traffic laws assume the moral principle of respect for life and property. Obviously, someone who drove the wrong way down a busy freeway would have respect for neither life nor property. Martin Luther King Jr. made the famous statement that "the law can't make people love me if they hate me because of my race. But the law can stop them from killing me."[3]

Let's also be clear about what we *should* legislate. Not every aspect of morality ought to be the subject of the law. Remember that the law is a very blunt instrument that often produces unanticipated consequences. Many things that are immoral are not illegal—for example, some sexual behavior among consenting adults, forms of lying and deception, and many character vices, such as gluttony, jealousy, drunkenness, greed, malice, and arrogance. Some things are not illegal because the law couldn't be enforced without intolerable invasions of privacy. Others are not illegal because no social harm is being done, particularly when involving consenting adults. In general, the law should get involved when significant harm to others results from behaviors under consideration, when fundamental rights are at stake, or when significant injustice can be prevented. This is why, for example, the law should get involved when fraud occurs and why racial discrimination is correctly the object of the law. The law gets involved less frequently when harm to oneself is at stake, as is the case with laws requiring seat belts and motorcycle helmets. Sometimes, though rarely, the law mandates things that prevent offense, such as laws against public nudity and prostitution. Infrequently the law mandates things that actually don't prevent harm but bring a benefit to someone, such as laws requiring mandatory schooling. In addition, the law mandates a few things that bring a benefit to others, such as paying taxes to provide benefits for the community, like infrastructure and law enforcement.

Government is under the moral law. In fact, some of the best examples of government doing good occur when it responds to a moral challenge. Remember from chapter 2 that Martin Luther King Jr. held that there is such a thing as an unjust law and that people are obligated to resist it. He was arguing that there is a moral law, and even government is subject to it. Throughout history government has been challenged by courageous people who had a moral objection to the law. Of course their criticism had to be valid and they had to have a compelling claim that the government was in the wrong. Likewise, governments are under a higher moral law when it comes to conduct in waging war. Citizens can use the criteria for a just war in holding government and the military accountable for both the decision to go to war and the way warfare is conducted. During World War II, for example, British clergy were highly critical of their government for the bombing of civilian neighborhoods in Germany in response to the German bombing of London. More recently, criticism of government in the war on terrorism has focused on the use of indefinite detainment facilities such as the one at Guantánamo Bay and the use of extreme measures such as waterboarding to extract information from suspects.

Sometimes criticism of the law comes from within government itself, as was the case with the British member of Parliament William Wilberforce, who led a two-decade battle to abolish slavery in the British Empire in the late 1700s and early 1800s. Wilberforce based his fight against slavery on religious convictions that all human beings are made in God's image and possess intrinsic dignity. He saw how the slave trade degraded people, separated families, and often condemned slaves to death in transit because the conditions were so appalling. He led the fight in Parliament to ban slave trade against the commercial interests of much of the country. Over time he won over not only public opinion but also his fellow legislators. Oxford professor of colonial history Sir Reginald Coupland summarized Wilberforce's impact: "More than any man, he had founded in the conscience of the British people a tradition of humanity and of responsibility towards the weak and backward ... whose fate lay in their hands. And that tradition has never died."[4] Wilberforce's biographer Eric Metaxas put it graphically: "Before Wilberforce, a world power like Great Britain could do what it liked with the people of Asia and Africa, and for two centuries and more did, treating human beings as they treated dumb beasts or insensate resources like timber, hemp, and ore; but after Wilberforce, all that changed. What Wilberforce and his friends achieved was nothing less, indeed, than a moral revolution."[5] This was an example of a nation and a government struggling to do the right thing and to emerge as a more developed and more just society. And they did finally emerge as a more just society.

However, sometimes it can go the other way, as was the case with the moral collapse of Nazi Germany during World War II. Government and culture both took significant steps backward in terms of justice and morality. As a result, sometimes the exercise of moral courage carries big costs. Professor David Miller describes the heroism of Dietrich Bonhoeffer, who resisted the Nazis and eventually joined in the plot to overthrow Hitler, which eventually cost him his freedom and his life:

> Dietrich Bonhoeffer has and will inspire generations just like Martin Luther King Jr. has in this country. Bonhoeffer was an unlikely hero. His family was all secular scholars; he became a theologian. At age twenty-one, he received his first doctorate, and the Swiss giant theologian, Karl Barth,

called it a "theological miracle." He traveled the world as an articulate spokesperson. He left the mainstream German church and challenged the church to remain faithful to Christ, as it was co-opted by the Nazis. He began an underground seminary movement to challenge the Nazi domain, who had overtaken the church and was preaching Hitler as Lord and not just God or Christ as Lord. As a result, he was arrested, imprisoned in Tegel Prison, tortured, interrogated for a couple of years, wrote one of his greatest works that we know today, *Ethics*, which has been compiled later in bits and manuscripts that were smuggled out of prison. Ultimately, he gave his life, was executed, hung, in Flossenbürg prison camp, *eleven days before the Allied forces liberated that camp.*

Bonhoeffer was even part of the failed plot to assassinate Hitler (a severe but genuine moral conflict for him), but unlike Wilberforce, all his efforts failed to make any meaningful change in Germany, though his legacy of courage and faithfulness will remain for generations through his writings.[6] Bonhoeffer described what went wrong in Nazi Germany to cause the collapse of morality:

The great masquerade of evil has played havoc with all of our ethical concepts. For evil to appear disguised as light, charity, historical necessity, or social justice is quite bewildering to anyone brought up on our traditional ethical concepts (the Judeo-Christian heritage).... What lies behind the collapse of ethics *is the death of civil courage*, courage in the public square. Unless we have the courage to fight for a revival of wholesome reserve between man and man, we shall perish in an anarchy of human values. One may ask whether there have ever been, in human history, people with so little ground under their feet.

Professor Robert George summarizes Bonhoeffer's commentary: "And then he goes on to talk about the collapse of conscience. The idea of conscience is a 'stern monitor,' imposing on us duty, a recognition of duty, to do what's right, even in the face of power-ful temptations and incentives to do what's wrong." The erosion of conscience began, according to Professor George, with "*the abandonment of the sanctity of life ethic.* Not the killing of Jews or Gypsies or others; that eventually came. It began with the kill-ing of handicapped people, people who were considered inferior because they weren't of the physical or mental powers of other people. That's how it began. When the handicapped became con-ceived as 'useless eaters.' "

In the midst of this erosion of conscience, Bonhoeffer had no place for those determined to sit on the sidelines in the face of evil. He said it is "better to engage in trying to defeat evil and risk getting your hands dirty and later fall on your knees for the grace and mercy of God, than to sit on the sidelines and be proud of how clean your hands are."[7] Part of the ethical tension in public life is that in a broken, fallen world one must sometimes be content with being faithful or with limited objectives. Not every encounter with evil will go as it did for Wilberforce, with his cause eventu-ally being triumphant, or as it did for Martin Luther King Jr., who established new civil rights laws with enduring value. It may be that those in the forefront of the abortion struggle may never see *Roe v. Wade* overturned and the unborn protected by the law. Or those in the battle against human trafficking may only make peri-odic progress in protecting human beings from being enslaved. From a Christian worldview, the kingdom of God is begun but not yet completed, and being faithful to the task is more important than whether one ever finally succeeds here on earth.

GOVERNMENT AND JUSTICE

Government has a legitimate role in the promotion of justice, both preventing injustice and providing remedies when it occurs. Ensuring that victims of injustice are compensated for their inju-ries and losses is the clearest form of justice, known as "compen-satory justice." In the United States, this is largely done through the legal system, through what is known as the "tort system." In other parts of the world, this is accomplished more through higher degrees of regulation. A common criticism of the tort system in the United States is that it has gone out of control, with plaintiffs winning enormous awards far out of proportion to the injuries received. This can serve as motivation for filing frivolous lawsuits in the hope of cashing in. One solution to this abuse of the system is for the courts to prohibit paying punitive damages (amounts awarded to punish individuals or organizations for wrongdoing) to plaintiffs, thereby limiting what they can recover to compensatory damages only.

Justice also involves offenders being punished for breaking the law. This is known as "retributive justice" and is accomplished through the criminal justice system. Chuck Colson was reminded of this aspect of justice when he went to prison following his role in the Watergate scandal.

> When I checked into prison, there was a GS7 case worker who was checking me in, former special counsel to the president of the United States. He didn't seem intimidated. He said to me, "You know why you're here, Mr. Colson?" I said, "I think I do." He said, "You're here to be punished." That's exactly right. That's what punishment is: a response to be sure that the victim is remedied and that the scales of justice are balanced.

That's not the sole purpose of the criminal justice system. It also is aimed at reform so that criminals don't return to prison once they are released.

The most complicated and controversial component of justice is what is called "distributive justice." Professor George defines it like this: "It's justice in the distribution of … the benefits and burdens of society." Distributive justice refers to how the goods produced by society are to be distributed and how that distribution is paid for. One common example of distributive justice involves the safety net for the poor, especially for those who cannot work to support themselves. It is widely accepted, and grounded deeply in the Bible, that the community is responsible for supporting those unable to take care of themselves. In the United States that was largely done by nongovernmental organizations (NGOs) such as the Salvation Army, churches, and extended families until the New Deal era of the 1930s. Though those entities are still vibrant in the United States today, government has taken over a larger share of caring for those in need. In Europe government has an even greater role and a correspondingly lesser role for voluntary associations in providing this safety net. Critics of government's role insist that as the state takes over more responsibility for the safety net, it crowds out nongovernmental institutions and organizations. A good argument can be made that the more local the provision of the safety net, the more efficiently it can be provided. That is, given similar resources, local charitable organizations can feed, clothe, and house more people more effectively than can the government, especially at the federal level. The difficulty with that is that the resources available to nongovernmental organizations are dwarfed by the needs of the poor, and it seems only the government has the necessary resources. One solution that would make more resources available to more local NGOs would be to allow individuals a tax credit instead of a tax deduction for contributions to organizations that address the needs of the poor in the community. Though this would take some resources out of the hands of the government, it would likely deploy them more efficiently at the local level.

Provision of a safety net for the poor utilizes one specific criteria for distributive justice — that of *need*. But that's not the only basis on which the benefits and burdens of society are distributed. We also distribute the benefits of society on the basis of *merit*, that you get what you earn. For example, if people work hard, get an education, and make good choices, we generally say they are getting what they deserve when they make more money than their counterparts who dropped out of school, are lazy, and don't apply themselves. At times merit is strictly financial and refers to the *ability to pay*. This is frequently the way the benefits of society are distributed in a largely market-oriented culture, though most agree there are some things for which ability to pay ought not be the trump card.[8] For example, most people agree that we ought not have an open market for adoptable children or organs for transplant, that we are better served by the "first-come, first-served" system now in place.

Sometimes we also invoke the opposite of merit, which we call *desert*, the principle that "you reap what you sow." *Equality* is sometimes invoked as criteria for distributing the benefits of society, though we generally refer to equality more in the realm of fundamental rights than the benefits of society. In general, we tend to distribute most of the goods of society on the basis of merit but rightly invoke need for those who cannot provide for themselves.

The current debate over health care reform is fundamentally a discussion of distributive justice — how the benefits and burdens of providing health care are to be distributed. Here, the criterion of need is more prominent, though at present the US health care system is a blend of need and ability to pay. How these two criteria are weighted relative to one another is the central issue of this debate. Those who advocate more market-based approaches focus on the ability to pay as the mechanism for obtaining health care, and their objective is to utilize market mechanisms such as competition to make health care more affordable. For example, proponents suggest allowing insurance companies to compete across state lines, which will result in bringing insurance costs down. They also suggest viewing health insurance in the same way we look at other forms of insurance, as protection for catastrophes, not a means of payment for all necessary services. They argue that we don't expect our auto insurance to pay for oil changes and other routine maintenance of our cars. They suggest that this must be accompanied by expanding and incentivizing medical savings accounts in order to help pay for the routine maintenance of our bodies. Those who advocate for this position tend to see health care more as a commodity, comparable to housing and food, for which we primarily use ability to pay as the means of distribution, but also distribute health care on the basis of need for those who cannot procure it for themselves.

However, those who advocate a more government-oriented approach tend to focus on need as the fundamental criteria for providing health care. They argue that competition can force down prices for many elective procedures, as it has done for LASIK surgery to correct nearsightedness and for cosmetic surgery. But they insist that acute care is not like that. When you need medical care immediately, you don't have the luxury to look around for the most competitive price for the needed services. They tend to see health care more as a right than a commodity, which suggests it ought to be provided to those who have need regardless of the cost.

It seems likely that in the United States, health care will continue to be distributed using the combined criteria of need and ability to pay, or what some call "market merit." It is important to be mindful of what exactly it is we are expecting our health care system to accomplish. Generally, we expect at least the following four things out of our health care system — high (if not world class) quality and innovation, universal access to care, full freedom to choose physicians, and low cost. But those are incompatible goals that cannot all be achieved at the same time. In the United States we have high-quality care (though the outcomes for health are lower than those in other countries that spend far less per capita on health care) and relatively high freedom to choose physicians (if you choose to go outside of your insurance network, you can do so), but access is far from universal, and costs continue to soar. Countries in Europe have universal access and low costs but pay high costs in terms of wait time for services and have little freedom to choose physicians and variable quality of care. Weighting of the criteria of need and ability to pay is important, but any health care system must make choices in the more specific goals it pursues and how it prioritizes them.

Education is also a topic of debate for which distributive justice is relevant. A major discussion is under way about how the good of education should be distributed and on what basis. This is an area where the criterion of *equality* is important, as evidenced by the lament of parents who have children in failing schools, that their kids *deserve* better, that they deserve a quality education because that's such an important starting point for success in life. If someone falls behind because of a poor education, it is considerably more difficult to make up for lost time and be successful than if that person's education is a good one. This is part of what is meant by the phrase "equality of opportunity," as opposed to "equality of outcome." Education is deemed a vital part of a level playing field from which everyone begins, and what they do with it will in part determine where they end up. As a result, we commonly say it is *unfair* for kids to be in substandard schools and thus fall behind at the very start. To be sure, we also recognize there is nothing unfair about those with financial resources using them to supplement their children's education with things like SAT preparation tests, tutors, Kaplan courses, and other extracurricular activities, such as overseas travel and access to museums. Attempts to remedy inequalities, such as a variety of affirmative action programs, should begin as early as possible and not wait until college or graduate school.

When it comes to higher education, merit becomes more prominent, though making college accessible to all is highly valued. But that doesn't mean everyone should have a free ride to elite universities such as the Ivy League schools or Stanford. We still acknowledge that merit and ability to pay are appropriate criteria for the distribution of scarce spaces at universities. However, the sensitivity toward adequate financial aid and the concern about rising student loan debt indicate some uneasiness with using ability to pay as the sole, or even primary, criteria for accessibility to higher education. When it comes to postgraduate education, the focus is almost entirely on merit, as need and equality, correctly, have little do with entrance to graduate and professional schools.

CONCLUSION

In this chapter, we have seen that ethics is not just for one's personal life. Those who serve in governmental positions are accountable to the moral law just as are those who work in health care or the marketplace. We have seen how government can and should be a force for good in society, that its roles include preserving order, ensuring justice, and promoting human flourishing, a blend of the Augustinian and Thomistic traditions. Thankfully, the American founders did not need to rely on the totalitarian solutions of Hobbes and Rousseau, because they were confident that the religious roots of American democracy provided a means of restraining individualism and the pursuit of self-interest. Government has a role in fostering a just society, which includes compensatory, retributive, and distributive justice. Government programs and services are not to replace voluntary associations such as the family, religious organizations, and private charities, and we saw that a good case could be made for giving priority to local means of meeting needs as opposed to the federal government doing so.

The cynicism in the culture about government and its ability to do good makes this discussion very important in our application of ethics to pressing issues of the day and current institutions. But this also involves strengthening mediating institutions that stand between the individual and the state and provide much of the moral training necessary to maintain civil society. Thus a part of government's role is to strengthen and empower these institutions that stand in the middle, particularly the family. This is because, as I have argued throughout these chapters, moral training begins in the family, where a person's moral compass is formed. I am not saying that people who don't grow up in stable families necessarily have a damaged moral sense, only that the place where much of the most powerful moral modeling takes place is at home.

Conclusion

We have seen a moral breakdown in the culture in general, evidenced by ethical failures at every stage of the financial crisis, the rise of the prison population, and the incoherence of how we think about morality — wanting to be relativists but unable to live with that philosophy consistently because we know there are many things that are just plain wrong. The person who holds a Christian worldview is not particularly surprised by this, given the reality of original sin that accounts for the existence of evil in the world. For a "reformation of manners" to occur, we must first recognize that there is such a thing as a moral law that can be known and is more than simply a matter of opinion. We distinguished between objective and subjective truths and concluded that morality is objective, should be regarded as knowledge, and is fundamentally different than people's preferences for flavors of ice cream. As a result, making moral assessments is entirely appropriate and necessary; otherwise culture will descend toward anarchy, which is where it inevitably ends if no one has the right to judge.

But to know the moral law is not enough — we must also adhere to it by cultivating character and virtue. We recognized that this is to be done in community, not in isolation, and we underscored the centrality of the family as the place where moral training and education best take place. This is because they can start at a very early age and can also be effectively modeled by parents living out virtue for their children to see. Many institutions are important in nurturing virtue, but none more important than the family. This is why the breakdown of the family has such tragic consequences for the moral life of the nation, producing increasing numbers of young adults with damaged moral compasses.

We then applied the moral law to issues of life and death and saw that morality demands recognizing and protecting the inherent dignity and worth of all human beings regardless of their ability to function. We saw how these values are being consistently eroded in the culture with the trends toward infanticide, assisted suicide, and eugenics. We then defended the idea that from conception forward, all human beings are members of the human community with rights to life that merit protection. This also affects how we view people with disabilities, and we rejected the idea of the "useless eaters" made popular by the Nazis during World War II.

We also applied the moral law to the marketplace and argued that trust and virtue are critical components not only of a healthy, functioning economy but also of a flourishing civil society. To be sure, a properly working market system requires a political framework that includes the rule of law, private property, and incentives for entrepreneurial activity. We saw that businesses contribute to the common good in many ways simply by doing business well, and they should be committed to doing no harm to their communities. We also recognized that good ethics are often costly (but more likely to pay off in the long run), and that ethics are more than compliance with the law and regulatory standards.

Finally, we have seen that cultivating virtue is an essential part of what constitutes a good life. Chuck Colson put it this way in reflecting on the powerful final scene in Steven Spielberg's film *Saving Private Ryan*:

> It's the story of a soldier who was lost but then found, and of Captain Miller, his commanding officer, who took a bullet and saved his life, and is slumped against a tank and dying. He looks over at Ryan, the young twenty-one-year-old whose life he just saved, and with his dying gasps, urges him to live a good life. The scene immediately moves to

the graveyard where Private Ryan, now seventy, has come back to visit. He goes for the grave marker, kneels, finds Captain Miller's grave marker, and says this: "Every day I have thought of that conversation we had on the bridge. I have tried to live a life worthy of your sacrifice," and then he stands up and turns to his wife, and says with the most pained and plaintive expression on his face, "Have I been a good man?" That's the most probing question any of us can ask, and at some point in your life, you will ask it, and in that moment you come to terms with who you really are, as Ryan did that night at the grave marker.

From a Christian worldview, the motive for living a good life has more depth, to be worthy of the calling to which we have been called (Eph. 4:1), to be worthy of God (Col. 1:10), and to be worthy of the ultimate sacrifice that Christ made on the cross (Phil. 1:27).

Acknowledgments

It is a privilege to write this book to accompany the Doing the Right Thing film series, which was cowritten (with Robert George) and produced by Chuck Colson. As you may know, Chuck went home to the Lord on April 21, 2012. He had intended to write this volume himself but ran out of time. I'm deeply grateful that the Colson Center and Zondervan entrusted this project to me. My goal from the start has been to produce a book of which Chuck would have been proud, and I will leave it to you, the readers, to tell me if I have succeeded.

I'm very grateful to Madison Trammel at Zondervan for his early editorial direction and to Laura Weller for her expertise in the actual editing of the book. I'm grateful to you both for your efforts that made the book clearer, more readable, and more compelling. Also, thanks to Chip Mahon, John Stonestreet, and Taylor Rae for their insightful readings of early drafts and suggestions that clearly made the book better. Special thanks to the panelists in the film series and those who participated in the "launch" events for the film. These include Robert George, Michael Miller, Glenn Sunshine, David Miller, and host Brit Hume. You'll undoubtedly see some of your comments have made their way into the book. I was delighted to be included as a panelist in film sessions 4 and 5 and to participate as a panelist and speaker in most of the launch events.

Thanks to Zondervan and the Colson Center for their partnership in this volume and others to come. I'm especially thankful to Zondervan for the roughly twenty years that they have published my various works in ethics.

Notes

Introduction

1. See Eric Metaxas, *Amazing Grace: William Wilberforce and the Heroic Campaign to End Slavery* (New York: HarperOne, 2007). See also the film based on the book, *Amazing Grace*.

Chapter 1: We're in an Ethical Mess!

1. All quotes without endnotes are from the film series Doing the Right Thing. In many instances, I have added italics for emphasis.
2. Stephen Davis et al., *Cheating in School: What We Know and What We Can Do* (Malden, MA: Blackwell, 2009); David Callahan, *The Cheating Culture: Why More Americans Are Doing Wrong to Get Ahead* (Orlando: Harcourt, 2004).
3. James B. Stewart, *Tangled Webs: How False Statements Are Undermining America: From Martha Stewart to Bernie Madoff* (New York: Penguin, 2011), 9.
4. Melinda Tankard-Reist, *Getting Real: Challenging the Sexualisation of Girls* (Sydney: Spinifex, 2010); Jean Kilbourne and Diane Levin, *So Sexy So Soon: The New Sexualized Childhood and What Parents Can Do to Protect Their Kids* (New York: Ballantine, 2008).
5. James Davison Hunter, *The Death of Character: Moral Educa-*

tion in an Age without Good or Evil (New York: Basic Books, 2000), xv.
6. You can read Colson's Harvard speech at http://www.break-point.org/features-columns/articles/entry/12/9649.
7. Ibid.
8. To read more on relativism, see Francis J. Beckwith and Gregory Koukl, *Relativism: Feet Planted Firmly in Mid-Air* (Grand Rapids: Baker, 1998).
9. This is also known as the "Euthyphro dilemma." To read more on this, see David Baggett and Jerry Walls, *Good God: The Theistic Foundations for Morality* (New York: Oxford Univ. Press, 2011).
10. William Lane Craig, personal conversation.
11. See his book by the same title: J. Budziszewski, *What We Can't Not Know: A Guide* (Dallas: Spence, 2003).
12. C. S. Lewis, *The Abolition of Man* (New York: Macmillan, 1944).

Chapter 2: Is There a Moral Law We Can Know?

1. C. S. Lewis, "Men without Chests," in *The Abolition of Man* (New York: Macmillan, 1944). See the additional discussion of this essay in chapter 3.
2. This definition comes from Louis P. Pojman, *Ethics: Discovering Right and Wrong*, 4th ed. (Belmont, CA: Wadsworth, 2002), 275.
3. Russ Shafer-Landau, *Moral Realism: A Defence* (New York: Oxford Univ. Press, 2003), 23.
4. Ibid.
5. Ibid., 26.
6. E. O. Wilson, "The Biological Basis for Morality," *Atlantic Monthly*, April 1998, 54.
7. Ibid.
8. Ibid., 58.

9. Michael Ruse, "Evolutionary Theory and Christian Ethics," in *The Darwinian Paradigm* (London: Routledge, 1989), 262. Cited in William Lane Craig, "The Indispensability of Theological Meta-Ethical Foundations for Morality," http://after-all.net/.

10. Though today, with the increase in human trafficking, slavery is again on the rise.

11. William Lane Craig, "The Indispensability of Theological Meta-Ethical Foundations for Morality," www.reasonable faith.org/the-indispensability-of-theological-meta-ethical-foundations-for-morality, accessed April 1, 2013. Originally published in *Foundations* 5 (1997): 9 – 12.

12. Richard Taylor, *Ethics, Faith and Reason* (Englewood Cliffs, NJ: Prentice-Hall, 1985), 2 – 3.

13. C. S. Lewis, *Mere Christianity* (New York: Macmillan, 1947).

14. For other examples of philosophers who argue for this view, see Russ Shafer-Landau, *Whatever Happened to Good and Evil?* (New York: Oxford Univ. Press, 2004), 75 – 84; and Pojman, *Ethics*, 187 – 205.

15. Lewis, *Mere Christianity*, 34, italics mine.

16. Arthur Allen Leff, "Unspeakable Ethics, Unnatural Law," *Duke Law Review* 6 (December 1979): 1230, 1232.

17. George Mavrodes, "Religion and the Queerness of Morality," in Louis P. Pojman, *Ethical Theory: Classical and Contemporary Readings*, 3rd ed. (Belmont, CA: Wadsworth, 1998), 653.

18. Leff, "Unspeakable Ethics, Unnatural Law," 1249.

CHAPTER 3: If We Know What's Right, Can We Do It?

1. Dallas Willard, *Renovation of the Heart: Putting on the Character of Christ* (Colorado Springs: NavPress, 2002), 16.

2. Stephanie Mehta, "Confessions of a CEO," *Fortune*, November 2, 2007, http://money.cnn.com/2007/10/30/new/newsmakers/confessions_ceo.fortune/index.htm.

3. Peter Kreeft, *Back to Virtue: Traditional Moral Wisdom for Modern Moral Confusion* (San Francisco: Ignatius, 1986), 30–31.

4. Robert Coles, "The Disparity between Intellect and Character," *Chronicle of Higher Education*, September 22, 1995, A68.

5. I'm indebted to my Colson Center colleague John Stonestreet for the material in this section on the way the culture attempts to nurture good people.

6. A number of books on this subject are available, chief of which is Alexandra Robbins and Abby Wilner, *Quarterlife Crisis: The Unique Challenges of Life in Your Twenties* (New York: Penguin, 2001).

7. Cited in Steven Garber, *The Fabric of Faithfulness: Weaving Together Belief and Behavior* (Downers Grove, IL: InterVarsity, 2007), 93.

8. Howard G. Hendricks, personal conversation.

9. C. S. Lewis, *The Abolition of Man: How Education Develops Man's Sense of Morality* (New York: Macmillan, 1947), 33.

10. Lewis, *Abolition of Man*, 34–35.

11. James Davison Hunter, *The Death of Character: Moral Education in an Age without Good or Evil* (New York: Basic Books, 2000), 226.

12. Ibid., 19. However, Hunter often sees faith communities as being co-opted by the dominant cultural views of morality rather than transforming them. With regard to evangelical Protestantism, he says, "That evangelical Protestantism, despite its public posturing to the contrary, is at least as comfortable with a therapeutic understanding of morality and moral development suggests once again that the resistance cultural conservatism offers to the dominant moral trends in America, may, in fact, be little resistance after all" (145).

13. Ibid., 225.

CHAPTER 4: What Does It Mean to Be Human?

1. See the story of Dr. Swan and Ken McGarrity, who were reunited in 1991, twenty-three years after Ken's injury and surgery, in Charles Colson and Nancy Pearcey, *How Now Shall We Live?* (Wheaton, IL: Tyndale House, 1999), 101 – 15.

2. Statistics from both the Guttmacher Institute and the Centers for Disease Control indicate this. See these figures at www.nrlc.org.

3. Judith Jarvis Thomson, "A Defense of Abortion," *Philosophy and Public Affairs* 1, no. 1 (Fall 1971): 48 – 59.

4. Ibid., 48.

5. Naomi Wolf, "Our Bodies, Our Souls," *New Republic*, October 16, 1995, 29, 32.

6. Ibid., 33 – 34.

7. Keith Pavlischek, "Paternal Responsibilities and Abortion Logic," *Capital Commentary*, December 7, 1998, http://www.cpjustice.org/stories/storyReader%24426, accessed December 17, 2012.

8. Cited in Joseph Bottum, "To Live and Die in Philadelphia," *Weekly Standard* 16, no. 20 (February 7, 2011), 16.

9. Ibid., 14.

10. Ibid., 18.

11. Ibid.

12. Alberto Giubilini and Francesca Minerva, "After-Birth Abortion: Why Should the Baby Live?" *Journal of Medical Ethics*, February 23, 2012, http://jme.bmj.content/39/5/26, accessed December 16, 2012, italics mine.

13. Richard Lamm, cited in Doing the Right Thing film series. See also "Gov. Lamm Asserts Elderly, If Very Ill, Have 'Duty to Die,'" *New York Times*, March 29, 1984, A16.

14. To be sure, there are some other European countries that do restrict PAS and euthanasia, such as Spain, France, and Germany.

15. Bruno Waterfield, "Euthanasia Twins Had Nothing to Live For," *London Telegraph*, January 14, 2013.

16. See the case of Buck v. Bell, 274 U.S. 200 (1927). It was overturned in Skinner v. Oklahoma, 315 U.S. 535 (1942).

17. "Gendercide: The War on Baby Girls," *The Economist*, May 4, 2010.

18. See, e.g., Jonathan Glover, *Choosing Children: Genes, Disability, and Design* (New York: Oxford Univ. Press, 2008).

19. See, e.g., Christopher Kaczor, *The Ethics of Abortion: Women's Rights, Human Life, and the Question of Justice* (New York: Routledge, 2011).

20. For further reading on this point, see Francis J. Beckwith, *Defending Life: A Moral and Legal Case against Abortion Choice* (New York: Cambridge Univ. Press, 2007).

Chapter 5: Ethics in the Marketplace

1. Brian Griffiths, *The Creation of Wealth: A Christian's Case for Capitalism* (Downers Grove, IL: InterVarsity, 1984), 52–53.

2. Dorothy L. Sayers, *Creed or Chaos? Why Christians Must Choose Either Dogma or Disaster* (Manchester, NH: Sophia, 1974), 72–73.

3. Michael Novak, *The Spirit of Democratic Capitalism* (New York: Madison, 1990).

4. Hernando de Soto, *The Mystery of Capital: Why Capitalism Triumphs in the West and Fails Everywhere Else* (New York: Basic Books, 2000).

5. Francis Fukuyama, *Trust: The Social Virtues and the Creation of Prosperity* (New York: Free Press, 1995).

6. To read more about the workplace as a crucible for a person's spiritual formation, see Kenman L. Wong and Scott B. Rae, *Business for the Common Good: A Christian Vision for the Marketplace* (Downers Grove, IL: IVP Academic, 2011), chap. 3.

7. Jim Wallis, *God's Politics: Why the Right Gets It Wrong and the Left Doesn't Get It* (New York: HarperCollins, 2005), 265.

8. Joseph E. Stiglitz, *The Price of Inequality: How Today's Divided Society Endangers Our Future* (New York: Norton, 2012), 1 – 2.

9. Charles Handy, "What's a Business For?" *Harvard Business Review*, December 2002.

10. Ibid., 51 – 52.

11. Dallas Willard, "The Business of Business," *Trinity Forum*, October 2006, www.dwillard.org/articles/artviews.asp?artID=161.

12. Ibid.

13. Handy, "What's a Business For?" 54, italics in original.

14. Jack Welch, quoted in Greg Smith, *Why I Left Goldman Sachs: A Wall Street Story* (New York: Grand Central, 2012), 179.

15. Albert Erisman, "Sherron Watkins: Did We Learn the Lessons from Enron?" *Ethix* 53 (June 2007), http://thix.org/2007/06/01/did-we-learn-the-lessons-from-enron.

16. William C. Pollard, "Mission as Organizing Principle," *Leader to Leader* 16 (Spring 2000), 4.

17. Ibid., 5 – 6.

18. Aleksandr Solzhenitsyn, "A World Split Apart," Harvard University commencement address, June 8, 1978, http://www.columbia.edu/cu/augustine/arch/Solzhenitsyn/harvard1978.html, accessed April 17, 2013.

19. John A. Byrne, "After Enron: The Ideal Corporation," *Business Week*, August 19 – 26, 2002, 68.

20. Amar Bhide and Howard H. Stevenson, "Why Be Honest If Honesty Doesn't Pay?" *Harvard Business Review*, September – October 1990, 121.

21. Ray Kroc, cited in Curt Schleier, "Ray Kroc's Overarching Dream," February 15, 2005, http://news.investors.com/management-leaders-in-success/021505-405437-ray-krocs-overarching-dream-build-on-success-he-franchised-one-small-idea-into-mcdonalds-monolith.htm, accessed April 17, 2013.

22. Joseph L. Badaracco Jr., *Leading Quietly: An Unorthodox Guide to Doing the Right Thing* (Boston: Harvard Business School Publishing, 2003), 9.

23. Donald Schmeltekopf, "The Moral Context of Business,"

speech given at Baylor University, 2003. Reprinted in Scott B. Rae and Kenman L. Wong, *Beyond Integrity*, 3rd ed. (Grand Rapids: Zondervan, 2012), 65.

Chapter 6: Ethics in Public Life

1. For further reading on these and other historical trends in political philosophy, see Greg Forster, *The Contested Public Square: The Crisis of Christianity and Politics* (Downers Grove, IL: InterVarsity, 2008).
2. These and many other citations from the American founders on the place of morality and religion in society can be found in A. James Reichley, *Religion in American Public Life* (Washington, DC: Brookings Institution Press, 1985), 53 – 114; quotes from 103, 112.
3. Martin Luther King Jr., quoted by David Miller in Doing the Right Thing film series.
4. Eric Metaxas, *Amazing Grace: William Wilberforce and the Heroic Campaign to End Slavery* (New York: HarperCollins, 2007), 273 – 74.
5. Ibid.
6. Bonhoeffer's main published works include *Ethics, Letters and Papers from Prison, The Cost of Discipleship*, and *Life Together*.
7. Dietrich Bonhoeffer, quoted by David Miller in Doing the Right Thing film series.
8. See, e.g., the provocative work by Harvard professor Michael Sandel, *What Money Can't Buy: The Moral Limits of Markets* (New York: Farrar, Straus, and Giroux, 2012).

Doing the Right Thing DVD

Making Moral Choices in a World Full of Options

Chuck Colson and Robert George, Hosted by Brit Hume

Doing the Right Thing explores the ethical and moral breakdown that is hitting culture from all sides. Through panel discussions, interviews, and live audience questions it raises ethical issues in a non-condemning but challenging way, stimulating thought, discussion, and action. The DVD sessions and accompanying participant's guide encourage viewers to examine themselves and how ethical and character issues relate to their lives at home, school, and the workplace.

As a result of this discussion and self-examination, participants will exhort each other and promote an ethic of virtue in their spheres of influence and in the culture at large.

This examination of ethics consists of six sessions, each designed to be completed in approximately one hour. Each session consists of approximately thirty minutes of video and thirty minutes of discussion.

Session topics include:

- How did we get into this mess?
- Is there truth, a moral law we all can know?
- If we know what is right, can we do it?
- What does it mean to be human?
- Ethics in the market place
- Ethics in public life

Available in stores and online!

ZONDERVAN®
.com

The Faith

What Christians Believe, Why They Believe It, and Why It Matters

Charles W. Colson and Gabe Lyons

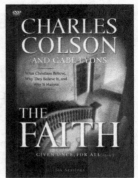

Through this six-session video-based small group study, *The Faith*, Charles Colson articulates the foundational truths of Christianity and how they compare to other belief systems.

The Faith small group Bible study will serve Christians—and non-Christians—for decades to come. Chuck Colson and Gabe Lyons lead you through six thought-provoking, soul-searching, and powerful sessions on the great, historical central truths of Christianity that have sustained believers through the centuries. Brought to immediacy with vivid, true stories, the truth of what Christianity is about and why it is a religion of hope, redemption, and beauty.

This DVD is designed for use with the companion participant's guide (sold separately). When used together they are a powerful catalyst for spiritual transformation.

Sessions include:

1. The Faith – Given Once and for All
2. What Went Right, What Went Wrong
3. The Free Gift – Costly Grace
4. The Trinity – God Above, God Beside, God Within
5. Be Holy – Transform the World
6. The Great Proposal

Available in stores and online!